Fort Calgary

100 YEARS

of

Smoke,

Sweat

and

Tears

By
Grant MacEwan
author
and

William Weisenburger, Project Co-ordinator
and Illustrations Editor

Entrusted to:

Firefighters Burn Treatment Society (Calgary Chapter)
The Firefighters Burn Treatment Society, Calgary Chapter, is a charitable organization raising funds for the promotion of education, medical research, rehabilitation and overall treatment of burn victims. The charity is carried on without purpose of gain for its members; any proceeds are used in promoting the objects of the society.

ISBN 0-88925-562-8

Published by
Calgary Fire Department
4124-11th Street S.E.
Calgary, Alberta T2G 3H2
Phone (403) 287-1150

Calgary Firefighters Association
538-7th Avenue S.E.
Calgary, Alberta T2G 0J6
Phone (403) 261-6966

First Printing, 1984

Printed and bound in Canada by
Friesen Printers
a Division of D. W. Friesen & Sons Ltd.
5720 Macleod Trail S.W.
Calgary, Alberta T2H 0J6

Head Office
Altona, Manitoba R0G 0B0
Canada

Dedication

To courageous firefighters of all generations who
have placed compassion and duty ahead of danger,
this volume is respectfully dedicated.

Introduction

The 100th anniversary of organized firefighting in the Calgary community deserves nothing less than a comprehensive review of the century of struggles and successes along with a tribute to the people who served as public guardians and brought honor to the fireman's badge and uniform. Of the importance of capturing and recording an historical record, there was never any question.

My role in this book project has been both pleasant and rewarding. Just as teachers stand to learn more about the subject at hand than pupils, so authors are likely to gain more than readers, and in compiling this record I have greatly enlarged my understanding of early Calgary where men of the Fire Department constituted a powerful and influential force. And, indeed, I have learned much about the prevention and suppression of fires, first in a small town and then in a fast growing city.

I knew I had much to learn about the science and practice of firefighting. As I explained to the friends who persuaded me to undertake the writing, my experience in dealing with burning buildings was primitive to the point of being funny. I confessed that the only firefighting success of which I could boast was in drowning a small blaze in a farm house attic with a bucket of buttermilk.

The farm neighbors across the road from the MacEwans saw smoke leaking from their attic and in a moment of panic, wasted all the water nearby by throwing it where it had no effect. When I arrived in response to their screaming call, the location of the fire between the kitchen ceiling and roof was clearly evident. I called for water and was told that none remained. Looking about the kitchen I spotted a pail of fresh buttermilk and seized it as I climbed the ladder to the hatch in the ceiling. The smoke was thick but the small flame was visible and I was lucky in directing the buttermilk at the right spot. The flame disappeared and before it had time to break out again, we had two pails of water from the well in the barnyard. The fire was out. I was pleased that my efforts may have saved a house but before I had time to congratulate myself, the lady of the house, without acknowledging my firefighting services, berated me for depriving her of her precious buttermilk.

The memory of that frontier encounter with fire, insignificant as it was in itself, should increase one's sense of appreciation for the advanced services and skills of today. Therein is a reminder, also, of progress and achievement with a distinct success story quality. That change in firefighting techniques and equipment rather parallels the story of mechanization in Western Canadian agriculture or the story of transportation that embraced scores of vehicles from Red River carts to high speed cars, trains and planes. In the case of the Calgary Fire Department, the story began with a volunteer brigade having a few buckets, some rope and two ladders and dealt ultimately with a million dollar department with one of the best firefighting records in the country. It's a story with which all Calgarians and all Albertans should be familiar.

My active involvement in the preparation of this book began with a telephone conversation in November, 1982. The caller, Firefighter William Weisenburger, informed me of his hope for a well illustrated history book on the Calgary Fire Department to be prepared and published in recognition of the one hundredth anniversary of firefighting in the community. He said he hoped I would help by, first, meeting to discuss the project and, second, by writing the narrative.

I hastened to assure him that in my opinion the idea of a book on Fire Department history was timely and excellent. I would be glad to attend the meeting but I was currently working on two manuscripts and would be unable to take on another writing assignment.

A few days later — on November 8th — I met with William Weisenburger and Jack Collison and, in the atmosphere of congeniality and overwhelming enthusiasm for the project, I could feel my resistance to the writing task melting like ice cream in summer sun. Before the end of our meeting, I was their submissive servant, almost instinctively pencilling proposed guidelines for the project.

Now that the book has become a reality, I have to say that the writing and related duties have been fun. No writer has ever found more willing helpers and more genial co-operation. Trying to name the individuals who were helpful could be dangerous because I wouldn't know where to stop. Notwithstanding the risks, I must repeat my thanks to William Weisenburger who as project coordinator and the person who did magnificently in assembling illustrations and records. Nor can I minimize my gratitude to Roy Shelley, Jack Collison and Harvey Moore, who as other members of the Book Committee I met from time to time; Fire Chiefs Frank Archer and Tom Minhinnett who were most generous with their support; former Chief W. D. Craig whose written recollections were offered freely; President Brent Pedersen of the Firefighters Association Local 255; Firefighters Gary Borkristl, Rick Choppe and Larry Fisher who gave of their time and skills to improve the range and quality of pictures; other officers, men and pensioners who came forward with recollections and old pictures, the Glenbow Alberta Foundation, Calgary Herald and Calgary Sun for unfailing readiness to share pictures and archival resources and finally the scores of unnamed friends who contributed in one way or another.

Grant MacEwan

Contents

Photo and Individual Credits

Photo Collections
Brooks, P. Mrs.
Calgary Firefighters Association
Calgary Fire Department
Calgary Fire Department Museum Group
Calgary Fire Department Pensioners
Calgary Firefighters Toy Association
Calgary Herald
Calgary Sun
Carr/Finlayson
Carter, T.
Dawson/Pow
Emergency Medical Services
Glenbow Museum
Glenbow Photo Archives
Kenting Earth Sciences Ltd.
Knight/Westrop
Lemieux, B. Mrs.
McLaughlin/Sinclair
Photo Sports Canada Ltd.
Robertson/Doherty
Romney, R.
Shelley, R.
Simmons/Barber
Tarrant
Wise-Buy Distributors

Book Title Contest Winner:
Mr. Gary Borkristl
100 Years Smoke, Sweat and Tears

Individual Contributors
Alberta Historical Foundation
Arbour, D.
Ashley, L.
Baillod, C.
Bartburger, E.
Beecher, I.
Binnion, R.
Borkristl, G.
Bothwell, J.
Brown, G.
Brown, L.
Buck, D.
Bunn, P.
Burdett, W.
Castleman, B.
Choppe, R.
Craig, D.
Crawford, R.
Dalton, D.
Davis, C.
Digney, J.
Dobbin, J.
Dougan, F.
Dover, M.
Dunsmore, D.
Eliuk, D.
Engen, D.
Fairhead, R.
Fisher, L.
Fitts, J.

Flaig, A.
From, D.
Fox, G.
Gilday, M.
Gregory, T.
Haden, G.
Hamilton, W.
Harrison, C.
Heard, K.
Henderson, J.
Hergert, D.
Hopkinson, C.
Hopkinson, P.
Hughes, S.
Jack, J.
Jeffery, G.
Kilroe, R.
Klassen, J.
Kruschel, W.
Lewko, J.
Lyons, A.
Markle, F.
Martin, W.
MacPherson, C.
McComb, W.
McDougall, J.
McIvor, D.
McLeod, J.
McRoberts, W.
Middleton, A.
Murray, G.
Nelson, D.
O'Dell, A.

Oelhaupl, F.
Parker, F.
Parrish, J. Mrs.
Pedersen, B.
Phillips, W.
Purnell, L.
Regan, W.
Reinders, J.
Reynolds, J.
Robb, D.
Rodger, D.
Rogers, J.
Saunders, L.
Senger, J.
Shearer, A.
Slobodian,
Spence, G.
Spotswood, K.
Spurway, K.
Stanley, J.
Steadman, R.
Strand, D.
Strang, N.
Stupak, W.
Sutherland, H.
Weisenburger, W.
Williams, H.
Williams, R.
Worden, B.

Centennial Book Project

Guide Line References
Bill Beattie
Jack Collison
Harvey Moore

Research and Support Group
Darlene Breckenridge
Peter and Roberta Bunn
Bob Devolin
Rick Fairhead
Garry and Sonia Hartle
Randy Kliewer
Eric Neilson

Phil Rosso
Roy Shelley
Heather Sutherland
Jan Weisenburger
Randy Yeats
Rob Yeats

Clerical
Joyce Avramenko
Marnie Barwell
Julie Van Seggelen
Lynn Jackson

Photography
Gary Borkristl
Rick Choppe
Larry Fisher

* Due to the excess of pictures, clippings and stories received, a second book "Milestones and Mementoes" is being compiled by the Centennial Book Project Committee and co-ordinated by B. Weisenburger.

Our Second Book, Milestones and Mementoes, is the personal side of the Calgary Fire Department and is an accumulation of Newspaper Clippings, Photos, Personal Stories and Memories, Poems, Cartoons, current membership photos and Nominal Roll from 1885. Proceeds from this book will be used for the preservation of our Calgary Fire Department Heritage.

Wm. B. (Bill) Weisenburger
Co-ordinator
Centennial Book Projects

In The Beginning

Canadians should not need to be reminded that fire in the cookstove or furnace is one of mankind's best friends while the same burning force when out of control or in unwanted places can be the most merciless of enemies. In driving humans to instant panic and frenzy, there is nothing in the language to equal the one word shout of "Fire."

Pioneer settlers were well aware of the fire dangers to which they were exposed and did not overlook the importance of serving themselves by effecting the best fire prevention available to them under frontier circumstances. It happened again and again that people living in new settlements didn't even wait for municipal incorporation and self government before endeavoring on their own initiative to reduce the fire dangers. It happened often that a village's first organization and the first expression of community cooperation took the form of a volunteer fire brigade, sometimes handicapped by total lack of equipment except for a few buckets.

So it was in early Calgary where the plowing of a fireguard around the collection of shabby and shapeless shacks was the first organized undertaking and a volunteer bucket brigade, often hampered by distance from water, was next — even before the legal incorporation that came in November, 1884.

Local government at this place called 20th Siding — later Calgary — had its beginning at a very informal meeting at the Methodist Church, called by James Reilly, owner of the still-uncompleted Royal Hotel. It was in the first week in January and from the meeting came a committee with instructions to apply for incorporation and act in a caretaker capacity. Major James Walker chosen to be chairman knew exactly what was needed. Although acting without funds and without taxing authority, the committee, as soon as the frost was out of the ground in the spring, managed to obtain a fireguard consisting of 12 nicely turned furrows and then a small group of volunteers ready to carry water and perform other simple duties in the event of fire.

But 1885 was the more memorable year of action and anxiety across the West — even in the area of fire control. C.P.R. builders working from East to West and from West to East were gradually closing the transcontinental gap, bearing in upon Craigellachie where the last spike would be driven in November. Bringing the anxiety were the embers of rebellion

Atlantic Avenue (9th Avenue). Today Calgary Tower approximately centre of picture.

1

Early prairie fire.

smoldering in the Metis settlements along the South Saskatchewan, north of Saskatoon, and breaking into flame in March and April. Settlers had reason for alarm and home-guard activities came to all frontier communities, especially the ones like Calgary that seemed to be dangerously exposed to Indian attack from nearby reservations. For the youthful town with population of little more than 500 and still in its first 12 months of incorporation, home-guard had double the usual significance.

The month of January brought the first major fire and resulted in the home of J. L. Bowen being completely destroyed. It was described as a "$575 house," meaning that it was one of the better residences in the town and was without insurance. The volunteers did their best but, working without equipment other than buckets and being hopelessly far from supplies of water, their efforts, according to the press of the day, were "somewhat feeble." They tried to pull down and remove a lean-to structure in which the fire was believed to have started but without success. The only real successes were in removing the furniture from the house and placing a rope around a hen-house located a few yards from the residence and pulling it away, hens and all.

Citizens who assembled out of curiosity — as citizens of all ages have been eager to do — took to throwing snowballs at the flames and according to the press, were almost as effective as those who were passing pails of water from a town water tank "to Mr. Ramsay who was on the roof."

The editor of the Calgary Herald noted that: "If we wanted an illustration of how necessary a fire engine is for the town, the ludicrous scene of snowballing a blazing house to quench the flames would give it. In a few minutes it was seen how perfectly useless it was to try and save the house . . . In twenty minutes the house was burned to the ground and the initial Calgary fire was over . . . Mr. Cottingham who is an old New York fireman and knows what he is talking about, says that if two or three men with axes had been on the scene when the fire was first noticed, the house would have been saved."[1]

The Mayor and most of the aldermen were among the spectators and the editor guessed correctly that better fire protection would be on the council agenda at an early meeting.

Mayor George Murdoch who arrived from his native New Brunswick ahead of the rails in 1883 and then became the town's first harness maker, concluded that water in accessible places and reliable amounts was the prime requirement if homes and business premises were to be protected even measurably. He called for a report which reached the council early in March. Digging wells to a depth of 25 feet would cost $1.50 per foot. With cribbing and needed appliances including "anti-freezing pumps," the total cost per working well would be $87.

That was a lot of money and the august aldermen were not about to act with immoderate haste, but at the next meeting of the council, on March 11th, they debated the recommendations of the Fire, Water and Light committee and gave approval. The committee was instructed to select eight sites for wells that would best serve Calgary's business and residential districts and then call for tenders for the digging.[2]

It was reassuring to know that there were unfailing water supplies in the Calgary gravel and peering into the future, the members of the council committee added that when a fire engine could be secured, it would be useful to construct water tanks at each of the wells as safeguards against pump failures.[3]

By midsummer Calgary had the wells and the

View of Calgary, looking south, 1889.

council resolved to buy some better equipment, meaning rubber buckets, hooks, rope and better ladders. The new luxury piece would be a two-wheel push cart for the ladders. The town would be obliged to depend until a later date upon volunteer firefighters but enthusiasm for better protection was growing and the time had come to give those who were loyally responding to the sound of the fire bell some official or legal status. Making more history than they realized, interested members of the community met on the evening of August 24, 1885, and organized the Calgary Hook, Ladder and Bucket Corps under the authority of Bylaw No. 3 of the town and gave the proud and famous Fire Department of later years an acceptable birthday date.

Doubt lingered about the exact date of that birthday meeting but the Calgary Herald in its issue of September 2nd, gave the essential information as follows: "At a meeting held in the Masonic Hall on the 24th [1885], a hook, ladder and bucket corps was organized under provisions of bylaw No. 3 . . . Twenty-two names were enrolled and Mr. Constantine was elected captain, Mr. E. Donohue as lieutenant and Mr. Grogan, secretary."[4]

Ladders, trucks and buckets, it was assured, would be obtained as quickly as possible and stored in a shed attached to the town hall for the present. Messrs. Clark, Millward and Soules were named to a committee for the purpose of enrolling more members and any person wishing to join was invited to advise the committee. But just days later, for reasons

never made clear, George Constantine resigned from the post of Captain and in an election which followed, Steve Jarrett assumed the position and the name of James Smart appeared with the rank of "hookman."

It probably came as a pleasant surprise that recruits to the Corps would now qualify for payments of 75 cents per man for each fire he attended. And, glory be, every cent of the revenue would be "take home pay" because there were no deductions and no such thing as income tax.

The same issue of the Calgary Herald gave assurance that the mayor and aldermen would not be laggards in furnishing new and better equipment as soon as the town could afford it. Mayor George Murdoch was sharing a letter from A. A. Andrews of Winnipeg, in which the writer was offering "to supply the municipality with a chemical fire engine for $1,100 and pay the duty on it, taking in return a note

The men of the old brigade in 1886.

George Murdoch's log shack, Sept. 3 or 4, 1883. L-R: McArthur, "a tender foot"; J. Grue, "an old trapper"; George Murdoch, first mayor of Calgary.

The mayor assumed the main responsibility of assessing public opinion and reported at a special meeting of the council on September 17, stating: "I am pleased to be able to state that with two exceptions the gentlemen who were spoken to on the matter expressed themselves as ready and willing to support the council."[6] But the price of the engine advanced to $1,600 plus duty, making a total of roughly $2,000. That was enough to produce further delay and further consultation with ratepayers. Finally, however, the council authorized the purchase and by the end of 1885, Calgary had a chemical engine being housed temporarily at Ford's livery stable, two dozen rubber buckets for which payment of $72 would be paid to the Toronto supplier as soon as the money was available, and the promise of new ladders as soon as Captain Jarrett could make a proper selection of pine poles from the mountains.[7]

for 12 months for the full amount, together with the duty."[5] Members of the council were clearly interested but hesitated about spending such a horrendous sum of borrowed money. Being more conscientious than many councils that followed, it was decided to defer until the wishes of the ratepayers could be ascertained.

[1] Calgary Herald, Jan. 8, 1885.
[2] Calgary Herald, March 12, 1885.
[3] Calgary Herald, March 5, 1885.
[4] Calgary Herald, Sept. 2, (Wed.) 1885.
[5] Ibid.
[6] Calgary Tribune, Sept. 23, 1885. (Second issue published)
[7] Calgary Tribune, Nov. 25, 1885.

Early chemical engine.

The First Big One At Calgary

Big fire on 9th Avenue, Nov. 7, 1886. I. S. Freeze, J. Paterson and Grand Central Hotel building is foreground. Between Centre Street and 1st Street East.

Just as every child could expect to catch mumps or measles or both, so it seemed, every town or city could expect its "baptism of fire" in the form of a costly conflagration that burned out of control and lingered hauntingly in local memories. Chicago's famous fire of 1871 — said to have started when a cow kicked over a kerosene lantern — burned for two days and two nights and left 100,000 people homeless. New York, Pittsburgh, Philadelphia, and Boston had historic fires, and so did Halifax, St. John, Quebec City, Fernie and scores of other places. Calgary's memorable fire of early years was in November, 1886 and serious enough to leave the infant town in shock and disbelief.

As an incorporated urban community, Calgary was two years old and emerging from one full year of political turmoil. George Murdoch, beginning his second year as mayor, found himself in bitter conflict with the new and unpopular Judge Jeremiah Travis who tried to rule the town the way a grade four teacher would rule in the classroom. The impasse reached the point in early 1886 where one of Murdoch's aldermanic friends was in jail for doubtful cause; the editor of the Calgary Herald, Hugh St.Q. Cayley, was in jail for contempt of court after publishing an editorial that was critical of Travis; Murdoch was facing a heavy fine with alternative of jail and mayor and aldermen were being unseated as elected representatives. It meant that for much of the year the town was without a working council. But late in the year the Territorial Council authorized a special election and George Clift King was elected to the mayor's office. At about the same time, Calgary held its first agricultural fair, the forerunner of the famous Calgary Exhibition and Stampede.

5

Optimism returned and Calgary's growth began to resemble that of a milk-fed pumpkin. The fact was that Calgary was outgrowing its fire protection of even one year earlier. Ratepayers who seemed to agree, accepted an invitation to attend a special meeting at Boynton Hall on September 6. James Martin who had made a study of fire protection told the audience that a bucket brigade and a chemical apparatus were not enough. Needed was a power unit that would supply a stream of water under pressure so it could be directed with force against a fire.

Martin told his audience that they had three choices: the town could install a "hand engine" that would draw its power from a team of strong men working the pump; such a machine for use in conjunction with the town wells would cost about $500. For a thousand dollars, the town could have a bigger unit driven by horses on a treadmill. But most of all, he would favor a steam fire engine that could be hauled by a team of horses. Such an engine with appliances and a building in which to keep it would cost $10,000.

Of course, nobody would favor an expenditure of such proportions unless it would effect big economies but James Reilly made the pertinent point that if its adoption would cut fire insurance premiums significantly, it would be a good investment. Martin said the savings in insurance premiums might be as high as 25 per cent.

But Martin was in error on the cost of a steam fire engine. It happened that Mr. Ronald of Brussels, Ont., manufacturer of the Ronald steam engine, was in the West and had already proposed terms on which he would supply an engine for Calgary. The cost of an engine of medium size with appliances, two hose carts and 1,000 feet of hose would be $5,000 and Ronald would take payment in municipal debentures bearing interest at six per cent and maturing in either 10 or 20 years. And to make Calgary people take special notice, the seller was prepared to guarantee that the installation of such an engine would bring insurance rates down the full 25 per cent as Martin had suggested.[2]

The town council was interested but not to the point of instant action as a few local people were urging. A few citizens appeared to have a premonition of a big fire. The Calgary Tribune of Friday, November 5, 1886, carried an item of news concerning a terrible fire at Southampton, England, destroying 50 buildings and leaving 30 families without homes. For this news story appearing less than 48 hours before the town's great misfortune, the editor chose for his headline: "A Warning To Calgary."[3]

And then the fire demon struck with all its fury. It was November 7. It was six o'clock on Sunday morning — a sleepy hour in every community — when smoke was seen issuing from the back of the flour and feed store occupied by Parish and Son at the northwest corner of Atlantic Avenue and McTavish Street — 9th and Centre at a later date. With all possible haste the church bell was sounded to give the alarm and members of the volunteer group came at a run, one by one. But the fire, thought to have started in hay at the rear of the store, spread quickly and was soon out of control. The remaining hope was to prevent the fire from spreading to neighboring buildings. With a moderately strong west wind even that was not to be easy. Before many minutes, the flames had taken possession of two adjacent buildings, Lamont's tin shop and store and the Massey Manufacturing company warehouse. Still the fire was not to be contained. The Sherman hotel at the back of the Parish store was next, then the Union hotel across the street and from there eastward on Atlantic.

By what one editor called "a superhuman effort" and the use of wet blankets, James Reilly's Royal Hotel fronting on Stephen and McTavish, was saved and the I. G. Baker store, being of log construction, escaped the worst of the burning. The reasoning was that if the Royal hotel burned, most nearby buildings on Stephen would follow.

As the fire advanced eastward on Atlantic it became clear that nothing would stop it as long as it had wood fuel to keep it going. Citizens resolved to remove or destroy some of the buildings on the path of the flames, thereby creating a sort of fireguard that would either break or retard the fire's advance. Mortimer's bakery and Murdoch's harness shop were selected for the sacrifice. An attempt was made to remove the harness shop with dynamite but the effort was not well executed and failed. Ropes and axes were then brought to the task and the two buildings were literally dragged away in pieces.[4]

This removal of the buildings helped substantially to check the eastward sweep of fire and a surviving picture shows the easterly end of the devastation on the Avenue, marked by three standing structures carrying the names of I. S. Freeze, J. Paterson and Grand Central Hotel.

Then, as misfortune would have it, the wind shifted to the east and the fire began creeping westward, more slowly. Finally, after three exhausting hours the fire was within controllable proportions and firemen, Mounted Police from the Fort, members of the town council and other workers could begin to relax and count the cost. Fourteen buildings had been destroyed, including four stores, three warehouses, a couple of saloons and four hotels. The Calgary Tribune estimated losses totalling $103,200.[5]

Miraculously, nobody was injured but personal losses took many forms. A. Carey lost $500 in paper money that was in the pocket of his coat hanging in the Union hotel. J. L. Bowen remembered a keg of gunpowder that was placed in storage at the Baker store and, at much risk, dashed in and carried it out, thereby preventing an explosion that would have spread the devastation. Another merchant had 2,000 rounds of cartridges on his shelves and these kept up a cannonading as they exploded. But nobody was shot. And noteworthy was the experience of George Murdoch for whom this was a second encounter with a big fire. Although raised in New Brunswick, he was living in Chicago at the time of the awful holocaust there and lost his home and household effects.

From the early morning hours when the fire was discovered there was suspicion of incendiarism and when fire broke out again at the end of the day at the Patterson barn which was not close to the embers, citizens became sure it was the work of an arsonist. Mayor George King who had been working on the fire front much of the day, addressed an outdoor gathering of citizens and spoke with a touch of anger and frontier recklessness: "Citizens of Calgary who have an interest in saving your town from the torch of the incendiary, I call upon you to watch and patrol the streets all night, and if you find any . . . man setting fire to any building, I hand him over to you and you may deal with him as you like."[6]

The crowd broke into cheers with apparent agreement that anybody who would stoop to arson deserved to be "hanged or shot in his tracks." It was the temper of the times.

Most people tried to be helpful that day. The Mounted Police performed magnificently. Thoughtfully, the C.P.R. agent provided a locomotive and tank car for hauling water from the railroad reservoir in an attempt to augment the amount the men of the Hook, Ladder and Bucket corps could carry from the town wells.

But where was the chemical fire engine that the town fathers bought months earlier? It had been delivered to Calgary but its arrival apparently found the town short of cash and unable to pay the freight charges. Consequently, the engine was impounded and placed under lock and key in a local barn. But midway through the fire on that November morning, impulsive workers made bold to force entrance to the stable and bring the apparatus to action. It produced no wonders but might have served better if men knew how to use it.

Even before the ashes were cool, Calgary people were calling for a steam engine that would deliver a strong and steady stream of water. Keep the chemical unit and get us a steam engine to go with it, an editor was saying.

Riding the crest of the new wave of enthusiasm, the Hook, Ladder and Bucket Corps held a meeting at the Town Hall a few days later and proceeded with reorganization. The result was a brigade with two divisions, a ladder division and a hose division, and 30 men in each. Almost at once the town officials reopened discussions with Mr. Ronald about a steam fire engine of medium size. A telegram from the Mayor to Ronald indicated interest in the engine but not at the price stated. Ronald replied with the offer of the engine at $4,000 and two hose reels at $200 each. As a sweetener, Ronald promised a donation of $200 to a fund for the fire victims, if the deal went through. Members of the council, with some seasoned horse traders among them, would give Ronald a chance to do still better in price and before the end of November closed a deal for the engine and two hose reels at a price total of $4,000.[8]

Calgary's fire protection was improved but relations between aldermen and firemen deteriorated. A structure for the new equipment was needed and was provided from $125 set aside for the painting of the town hall. The new building was humble enough but it had a big sitting room with comfortable chairs and the aldermen, thinking they had a claim, took to using it for both meetings and place of relaxation. The firemen objected and resigned, taking care to sell the furniture before they vacated, giving the money to charity.

The aldermen, unwilling to surrender, appointed themselves as volunteer firemen and appointed an experienced captain. The arrangement was working well until Calgary had a big fire and the new aldermanic hands were so awkward that public demand brought the seasoned firemen back for reinstating. The firefighters were reassured of prior claim to their former premises and peace came again to the town's administration.

Fire at Boynton Hall, Stephen Avenue, Spring, 1887.

[1] Calgary Tribune, Sept. 11, 1886.
[2] Calgary Tribune, Aug. 7, 1886.
[3] Calgary Tribune, Nov. 5 (Fri.), 1886.
[4] Calgary Herald, Nov. 13, 1886.
[5] Calgary Tribune, Nov. 12, 1886.
[6] Calgary Tribune, Nov. 12, 1886.
[7] Calgary Tribune, Nov. 26, 1886.
[8] Ibid.

Early Memorabilia of Calgary Fire Department

Leather helmet.

Early city logo.

Medals, badges of the early brigade.

Cappy Smart's bugle, badge number 1 and watch.

Street and Avenue Names (Early Calgary) Prior to 1900's

Street	Old Name
Centre Street	McTavish Street
1 Street East	Osler Street
2 Street East	Drinkwater Street
3 Street East	Hardisty Street
4 Street East	Dewdney Street
1 Street West	Scarth Street
2 Street West	Hamilton Street
3 Street West	Barclay Street
4 Street West	Ross Street

Avenue's North of C.P.R. Tracks

9 Avenue	Atlantic Avenue (also known as Whiskey Row)
8 Avenue	Stephen Avenue
7 Avenue	McIntyre Avenue
6 Avenue	Angus Avenue
5 Avenue	Northcote Avenue
4 Avenue	Reinach Avenue
3 Avenue	Egan Avenue
2 Avenue	Abbott Avenue

Avenue's South of C.P.R. Tracks

10 Avenue	Pacific Avenue
11 Avenue	Smith Avenue
12 Avenue	Van Horne Avenue
13 Avenue	Kennedy Avenue
14 Avenue	Grenfell Avenue
15 Avenue	Rose Avenue
17 Avenue	Notre Dame Avenue

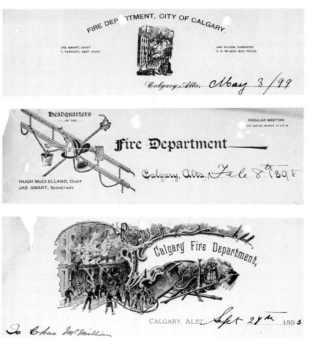

Early letterheads.

Galloping Hoofs On The Avenue

Galloping horses were not uncommon on Stephen and Atlantic Avenues. It was a relatively dull day that passed without a horse race conducted to settle a four dollar bet, and at least one spirited runaway, wild enough to fill spectators with fear. But when the town began to mature they were the trained horses rushing to fires that galloped most commonly along the streets and avenues — and into human hearts.

From the moment the Ronald steam-powered pumper was placed in service, horses were needed to pull it to the scenes of fire. The town council relied at first upon local owners of horse teams to respond instantly to the sound of the fire bell and travel with all possible haste to the place where the engine was stored, there to hitch to it and haul it to the burning.

The horseman who was first to reach the engine and delivered it at the scene of fire qualified for a cash payment of $5.00. That was the equivalent of ordinary wages for three days. The arrangement was satisfactory until two horsemen rushing to hitch to the engine arrived in a "dead heat" and while arguing and shaking fists at each other, a third teamster drove in and after making a fast hitch, drove away to qualify for the cash prize.

At the meeting on February, 11, 1890, Calgary's mayor and council raised the rate of payment for such horse services. Thereafter, as the decision was reported, the first horseman with team who arrived at the fire hall and then fulfilled his duty by hauling the engine to the fire and bringing it back after the fire would receive $10.00 while the second horseman in the race would qualify for $5.00 and the third for $3.00. [1]

Ronald steam pumper.

At the same meeting, the council gave approval to alterations at the fire hall to provide for the stabling there of three horses, two of them for use in connection with the steam engine and the third for the chemical cart. The volunteer firemen who were occupying sleeping accommodation at the fire hall had mixed feelings about sharing living quarters with horses but they accepted and upon admitting the first horses as full time boarders at the hall, there was an immediate incentive to train them for their jobs, much as the firemen would train themselves to increase their efficiency. The first horses installed had been dray horses or farm horses but with good training they soon became professionals and Calgary had some of the best.

Horse-drawn hose wagon at No. 6 fire station, 1913.

No. 1 fire hall, late 1890's. Erected in 1887. Located on 7th Avenue between Centre and 1st Streets East, on north side. Calgary Feed and Livery stable in foreground. "Cappy" Smart's house to left of fire hall.

By the end of May, the three horses in residence were getting their "basic training" and responding well. An editor attended at an evening hour when the single horse allocated to the chemical cart was receiving its regular lesson. "The gong is sounded," the newspaper man wrote, "and the horse is hitched with all possible dispatch — about 14 seconds. The horse is getting to know his business quite as well as the men and on the first sound of the gong is ready and anxious to rush from the stall to the machine."[2]

After becoming Chief in 1898, James "Cappy" Smart personally selected the horses for the Department and was so successful in choosing and training fire horses that he was being asked often to buy or recommend horses for similar needs elsewhere.

When distinguished visitors came to Calgary, the mayor was likely to ask the Chief to conduct an exhibition run with one of his best teams. So it was when Prince Fushimi of Japan was in the city. For the guests edification and the mayor's satisfaction, a team from No. 1 Fire Hall responded to the signal,

dashed as usual into position to have harness dropped and fastened, then dashed almost a quarter of a mile on the city street to allow firemen to lay 150 feet of hose and have a stream of water playing on an imaginary fire, all within a minute and 25 seconds from the instant the gong sounded.

The best of the horses in the Calgary service were bought from foothills ranches like the Quorn where policy was to import high class Thoroughbred sires for use on range mares. Cappy Smart favored black horses but bought at least one team of matched greys and the famous grey mare, White Wings.

The inventory for 1911 showed 21 horses in service — 10 matched teams and White Wings, always the odd numbered animal because of her special assignment in pulling the one-horse chemical cart. Leishman McNeill, an authority on early Calgary and one who admitted to occasional school truancy to accommodate extra visits with the horses at the fire hall, related the well known incident attributed to White Wings.

The fire bell sounded; White Wings was buckled into her harness and Sam Saunders seized the reins but in leaving the fire hall in a burst of speed and making a short turn on a rough place on the street, the driver fell off. White Wings did not stop. The mare knew it was no time to stop. Her mind was on the fire and she simply followed the hose wagon ahead of her until she reached the scene of the fire where "she backed into position" for action. "Old White Wings," said McNeill, "didn't need a driver."[3]

Two of the well known Calgary fire horses won the hearts of additional hundreds of visitors when they performed in front of the grandstand on the occasion of the Dominion Exhibition in the city in 1908. By way of preparation for the unscheduled demonstration, a ladder wagon with harness suspended immediately in front — as in the fire halls — was placed in clear view of people on the bleachers. The two horses known as the Jack Rabbits were then released to graze on the infield grass.

At a given moment when the grandstand was full of unsuspecting customers, Cappy Smart sounded the fire gong that customarily brought the horses from their stalls to stand momentarily for their harness. On this occasion the grazing horses recognized the bell, raised their heads and looked around. Seeing the fire wagon, they dashed knowingly to it to stand for the harness to be fastened. Prancing nervously, they waited for Jack Smart — Cappy's brother — to climb to the driver's seat, then galloped away, encircling the track. On coming to a stop after the half-mile run, the fire horses were applauded like heroes, even though looking annoyed that they had been called to answer another false alarm.

Chief Cappy Smart loved horses and was properly proud of the ones occupying the fire hall stalls. But he was one of the first to recognize the advantages of mechanization. By 1920, he was convinced that the horses had to be displaced. Gradually, the horses were sold or retired but they never lost interest in fire bells and the urge to be going. A Calgary fireman with long experience in driving the horse-drawn vehicles, told about the aging team sold to a nearby farmer for use in doing chores. The horses

No. 2 fire station on 12th Avenue, 1905.

11

were generally quiet and contented but as the farmer discovered to his sorrow, they were capable of sudden transformation of mood at the sound of a fire bell.

It was his misfortune to be hauling a load of pigs to the stockyard and travelling on what he thought was a quiet street in East Calgary when a fire wagon with alarm bell clanging was heard bearing down upon him from the rear. Instantly, the two old horses became excited and wanted to run. The owner was able to restrain them until the fire outfit passed and then, suddenly, the old horses were young horses again, going to the fire, and nothing would stop them. The wagon bounced and rattled on the stone-strewn road and one pig was thrown out of the wagon box. The driver thought he would be next to be thrown but, finally, upon reaching the place of the fire, the two old horses stopped and stood quietly, evidently satisfied that they had done their duty again.

When horses from the fire halls were sold or retired, Cappy Smart tried to place them near the city so that he might see them from time to time. They were still his friends. Syd. Hughes who joined the Calgary Fire Department as Smart's chauffeur in 1914 and remained in service until retirement with the rank of Battalion Chief after 38½ years, recalled

the last two horses to be retired. They were greys, Charlie and Champ, 19 and 22 years old respectively, and were sent to a farm near Midnapore where good grazing seemed to be assured.[4]

But when the Chief, some time later, drove to the farm, he was shocked to find the horses looking hungry and neglected. He wondered: could it be that these old horses that had spent their lives in firehalls had never grazed and were now too old to learn and adjust? In any case, he ordered their return to the city and placement where they would be sure of hay and oats and a bran mash on Saturday nights.

It was a sad day for the lovers of fire horses when the last of them were retired in 1933. The change had to come in the name of efficiency but in the words of Leishman McNeill, much of the glamour and sentiment of the years departed with the horses. "The old horses that we as children loved so well — Jimmie and Squibby, Dick and Frank, Bob and Brownie, and the one we thought the grandest of all, Old White Wings — were no longer needed; they had served their day and were retired to a well earned rest."[5]

[1] Calgary Tribune, Feb. 12, 1890.
[2] Calgary Tribune, May 28, 1890.
[3] McNeill, Leishman, Tales of the Old Town, p. 28, published by Calgary Herald, 1950.
[4] Hughes, Syd, Interview, Calgary, Jan. 16, 1983.
[5] McNeill, Leishman, Tales of the Old Town, p. 27, Calgary Herald, 1950.

No. 1 fire hall, late 1880's.

Chemical No. 1, Calgary Fire Department

Hose Reel No. 2, Calgary Fire Department

Particulars of Calgary Fire Department Horses

	Name	Height	Weight	Age	Colour	Purchased	On Duty
1.	Cap (Shorty)	15.3	1150	16 yrs.	Bay	1904	Relief Duty Old No. 2
2.	Pete	16.	1300	16 yrs.	Bay	1904	No. 3 Station
3.	Frank	17.	1500	21 yrs.	White	1906	No. 3 Station
4.	Baldo	15.3	1300	14 yrs.	Bay	1906	No. 7 Station
5.	Mac	15.	1300	11 yrs.	Bay	1909	No. 3 Station
6.	Jack	16.2	1400	14 yrs.	Black	1910	No. 3 Station
7.	Nigger	15.3	1300	11 yrs.	Black	1910	Relief Duty No. 2
8.	Coon	15.3	1300	10 yrs.	Black	1910	Relief Duty No. 2
9.	Carbon	16.	1400	10 yrs.	Black	1912	No. 2 Station
10.	Bob	16.	1400	9 yrs.	Black	1912	No. 2 Station
11.	Major	15.2	1300	7 yrs.	Bay	1913	No. 9 Station
12.	Dick	15.2	1300	7 yrs.	Bay	1913	No. 9 Station
13.	Mike	15.	1300	7 yrs.	Dark Brown	1913	No. 7 Station
14.	Charlie	16.1	1300	6 yrs.	Grey	1913	No. 4 Station
15.	Champion	16.2	1300	7 yrs.	Grey	1913	No. 4 Station

Frank Died February 1915.
Mac was discharged June 1917.
Pete Died April 1918.
Charlie and Champion were pensioned off at the age of 26 and 25 respectfully. They were put to grass on Dewdney Estate, Glenmore Dam, May 13, 1932. On March 7, 1933, Charlie and Champion were loaned over to Mr. A. Sales 2339-16A Street S.E. and were shipped to his farm for light work.

Decorated Apparatus For Parades

Advancing With The Times

Fire department personnel and equipment, 1900.

Emperor Nero — last of the Roman Caesars — should have drawn some useful lesson from his folly and declared proverbially that a man can't fight a fire with a fiddle.

The spectacular advancements from the volunteer brigade technique, well known in early Calgary, to the highly specialized and sophisticated equipment in use in modern fire fighting were comparable to those seen in western grain fields where the sweep of change was from scythes and reapers to self-propelled combines in little more than an average span of human life.

The primitive metal or rubber buckets in the hands of members of the Volunteer Bucket Brigade served acceptably as long as there was nothing better available but in a serious test as on November 7, 1886 when Calgary had its first big fire, the buckets proved totally inadequate. It was perfectly clear that protection from fire and fire losses demanded alarm systems, reliable water supplies, the use of chemicals as fire suppressives, better ladders, water pressure furnished by pumps or gravity lines, the best possible

training for men entrusted with fire control and instant responses by trained horses as well as men.

The Town Council's decision in 1887 to build a proper fire hall and headquarters was well received by citizens and the formal opening on the 24th of May was marked with a dance. It was Calgary's first No. 1 Firehall and was situated on the north side of McIntyre Avenue — now 7th — close to the site upon which the Royal Canadian Legion was built later. Its most imposing feature was its bell and hose tower rising higher than most church spires. With sleeping accommodation for a certain number of men, a few of the volunteers accepted the invitation to move in and make their home at the hall. And at the rear of the building the first fire horses — a rented team — were stabled.

This was the structure which, with better fittings than the town hall, generated the quarrel of the year between members of the town council who had authorized and financed the fire hall and believed they should have the right to its use for meetings, and the firemen who resented the aldermanic intrusion and

ited but the Ronald steam pumper, a double cylinder chemical engine of 61 gallons capacity, three hose reels, 3,000 feet of two-inch hose, ladders made in Calgary by the Cushing firm, buckets, axes and other necessities "are all in good order."

The firemen, by this date, had the benefit of a team of horses which, by arrangement with the owner, was stabled beside the fire hall every night and in a trial run conducted at the inspector's request, the animals were found to be "well trained to the work."

The inspector took stock of the seven water tanks, well distributed to serve the community, and left the best description of the water situation at the time. Of the seven tanks, with total capacity of 71,000 gallons, two had been leaking and were being repaired. The others were full. "The tank at the fire hall," he wrote, "is filled from a well situated 40 feet to the rear, which is inexhaustible. A pump throwing 200 gallons per minute is attached to the well and worked by a windmill. The other tanks are filled by the fire engine from the tank at the fire hall."

The visiting expert was pleased to report four fire alarm boxes being installed. As he noted, Calgary at that time had a day telephone service but none at night; nevertheless, "all telephones are connected at night with the fire hall and the ringing of any one turns on the alarm."

As for the fire fighting personnel, Woodman saw "one paid engineer, one paid foreman and 30 volunteers. The volunteers are paid 50 cents an hour for fires and 30 cents for practice. Twelve men sleep in the fire hall."

told the Town Fathers that they could move in and assume full responsibility for fighting fires at 50 cents an hour or they could stay out. So great was the attraction of the new fire hall that the aldermen accepted the challenge to be part time firemen and the members of the volunteer brigade resigned. But as mentioned elsewhere, after an inglorious performance by the aldermanic firefighters at the first big fire, public demand brought the regular volunteers back to the fire hall and peace returned to the civic scene.

The Calgary Fire Brigade, in November, 1889, came under the first adjudication from the outside when G. O. Woodman, an inspector for the City of London Fire Insurance Company visited Calgary to conduct the formal inspection. It might have been expected that the visitor would be highly critical of this frontier effort. On the contrary, he found reasons for compliments. The fire hall of brick veneer, he said, was well located and well arranged and had a first class tower and alarm bell. He probably wondered how the 1500-pound bell had been hoisted to its commanding position in the tower.

Appliances, he reported honestly, were still lim-

Calgary Fire Brigade, 1900. Front Row, L-R: Tom Smart, Alex McTavish, B. Laycock, Billie Meldran, John McCaffrey, Tom Bruce, Ed. C. Hall, Everett Marshall. Second Row: James Fletcher, Tom Tarrant, George Mitchell, "Cappy" Smart, Charles Traunweiser, Wm. Zeigler, "Scotty" Lloyd. Third Row: Fred Tarrant, Billy Corcoran, Julian Smart, Louis Augade, Charlie Coleman, Hiram Worden, Neil McLaughlin. Others in rear: R. Bagley, G. Poneton, W. Thornton, H. McLellan, M. Morrin, Ike Saunders, A. Bassatt, W. Hickling, M. Costello, V. Ridley, E. Fletcher, H. Wilson.

Concluding his report — which must be seen as the most comprehensive and most reliable to come from the period of 1890 — the inspector wrote significantly: "At my suggestion, an alarm was turned on and a run of close to a quarter of a mile given to the tank at the corner of Scarth Street and Stephen Avenue. In five and a half minutes after the alarm was sounded two streams were thrown over the Alberta Hotel, a three story building. There was no delay or confusion amongst the men in getting to work and they appeared well trained and well managed."[1]

That was the report from 1890 and may have been the most accurate written up to that time.

force. More young men wanted to join and more firemen — old and young in service — found new pride in their jobs, pride in the high state of physical fitness which was demanded as a condition of recruitment and encouraged constantly, and new pride in the Calgary Fire Department's Band. Firefighting was still conducted on a volunteer basis but the fraternal feeling was growing. It was a mark of maturity and pride when the men of the force, late in that year of '98, bought their own uniforms, 30 of them at $18 per suit, paying for them from their personal savings.

A short time later, in 1902, the Calgary Firemen's

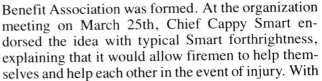

Operational stream display.

"Cappy" James Smart's elevation to the rank of Chief in 1898 proved to be a landmark in the history of the brigade and the life of the city, leaving that year to be remembered for something more than a goldrush to the Yukon. It brought fresh vigor to the entire

Benefit Association was formed. At the organization meeting on March 25th, Chief Cappy Smart endorsed the idea with typical Smart forthrightness, explaining that it would allow firemen to help themselves and help each other in the event of injury. With

James "Cappy" Smart appointed chief, March 21, 1898.

Calgary parade on 8th Avenue East, May 24, 1901. Looking west from 1st Street East. Calgary fire department band on parade.

bigger buildings in a bigger city, he said, risks and dangers would not diminish. Organization proceeded with membership fee set at $2.50 per person and a promise that the fund would pay up to $20 per month in case of injury and $50 toward funeral expenses in the event of death. It was a comparatively new concept at the time but 35 firemen joined and the organization gained respect and permanency.

Effective fire fighting demanded rapid early action and the alarm system was expanded and improved. Where there were four street boxes when G. O. Woodman reported, the number rose to 56 when the new Gamewell alarm system was installed in 1910. To supplement the telephonic alarms were 13 well placed fire bells, including the 1500-pound monster that hung high in the tower at No. 1 Fire Hall and pealed loud enough to be heard almost right across the city.

Gamewell alarm, box system.

But the most evident advancements were those in equipment. The science and practice of dealing with fire were changing and Cappy Smart was ever on the forefront of change. He was one of the first to adopt motor vehicles and sense the complete abandonment of horses in the service. By 1903 all Calgary fire rigs were carrying small or portable chemical extinguishers and in the next year, the City bought, first, a new and bigger chemical wagon and then another steam pumper, this time a Waterous of 800 gallons capacity. In 1905, also, came Calgary's first aerial ladder rig, a Seagrave horse-drawn vehicle with ladders that were hoisted by means of hand cranks. Its appearance created almost as much Stephen Avenue discussion as the birth of the Province of Alberta about the same time.

By 1909 and '10, the pace of change was quickening. A new gravity water system was completed in the former year by which water was conducted by a 30-inch flume for 11 miles to be deposited in a relatively high reservoir near Currie Barracks. Thereafter, firemen had the benefit of greater water pressure. Simultaneously, the time-honored volunteer system of furnishing manpower was finally abandoned. Calgary, for the beginning of the second decade of the century had a brigade of full time and fully paid firemen.

Three new fire halls were added and Cappy Smart's "Firecrackers" as the men were often called, were brought to a total of 40. Nor was it to be overlooked that 1910 brought the organization of the Dominion Association of Fire Chiefs, another organization for which Chief Cappy Smart had pressed.

And then came the decade of World War, manpower shortages, the memorable Burns plant fire and the dramatic shift toward motorization of fire fighting equipment.

---

[1] Woodman, G. O., The Efficiency of the Calgary Fire Appliances, Calgary Tribune, Jan. 22, 1890.

Cappy Smart's "Firecrackers."

Waterous steam pumper.

Horse drawn aerial.

FIRE HALL No. 3.

FIRE HALL No. 1.

FIRE HALL No. 2.

CALGARY, ALTA.

Fire Hall No. 1.

Chief Smart. Calgary Fire Department.

Aerial Truck, Calgary Fire Department

Hose Reel No. 1, Calgary Fire Department.

Captain Blood Of The Brigade

James "Cappy" Smart.

If Calgarians in the first decades of the present century had been asked to identify their local heroes, most would have named James "Cappy" Smart, the man who refereed the boxing matches, started the annual road races, served as a sort of perpetual Parade Marshal for the Exhibition, promoted sports and physical fitness and ran the best fire department in the country.

Even boys old enough to indulge in hero worship would have chosen Cappy. Leishman McNeill who spoke with authority about early Calgary, said that Cappy's image left most boys dreaming about becoming firemen. For the city, the Cappy Smart influence was like that of a one-man Board of Trade and Publicity Bureau. Everybody knew him and if the Foothills City of the time offered an annual award for the most newsworthy citizen, Cappy would have won it with the unfailing regularity of Canada geese flying south in the autumn.

Some observers said he was rough and tough but the pioneers who admired vigor and versatility, admired Cappy. They were reassured by the excellent record in fighting fires and they were entertained by Cappy's style and originality. They laughed in 1917 when, in the face of allied reverses on the European war front, Cappy said that if things got any worse over there, he would be obliged to put army clothes on his firemen and take them to Europe to capture the Kaiser and restore peace.

They laughed when Cappy remarked that he had no fears about the heat in Hell when his time came because many members of his Calgary Fire Department would be there ahead of him and they'd have the flames of Satan's overheated furnaces under such control that temperatures would be down to comfortable levels.

Smart was indeed a pioneer, having come to Calgary in 1883 — the year of the rails — and come to stay. It was indicative of his popularity with the pioneers when he was elected to serve as President of the Calgary Exhibition Board in 1906, President of that elite body, the Southern Alberta Pioneer's and Old Timer's Association in 1930, to say nothing of numerous presidential posts in Canadian and North American firemens' organizations.

James Smart was born at Arbroath in Scotland on July 12, 1865. He might have taken to the life of a seaman — like his father — but he would see Canada first. Schooling was limited and in early 1883 he was in Winnipeg, looking for a job. There he learned something about the mortician's profession but he didn't stay long and, in the company of an uncle, travelled as far as Calgary on one of the first passenger trains to go that far on the new rails. Still ready to accept the first job offered, the young fellow hired with Major James Walker who had a sawmill. While piling lumber, he was also cultivating a lifelong friendship with his employer.

James "Cappy" Smart dressed as Sir Harry Lauder, Scottish comedian.

With a premonition that he was in Calgary to stay, he was not overlooking the possibility of going into business for himself. He decided to open an undertaker's parlor. It would not be a thriving business in a community where almost everybody was young and the only deaths were from violence and freezing in winter blizzards, but it would pick up.

The undertaking parlor was located on the north side of Stephen Avenue, a few doors east of McTavish or Centre Street and, according to Leishman McNeill, next to a barber shop operated by a man who couldn't leave the bottle alone. When overcome by an alcoholic drowsiness, the barber would wander into Smart's parlor and lie down on the couch and go to sleep. When this had occurred too often and Smart had a new helper in his shop, he instructed the novice helper to prepare the body on the couch for a coffin and burial. The willing assistant went to work on the barber and had removed most clothing when the drunk awakened, dashed half clothed from the premises, shouting hysterically that he would never again venture into Smart's mortuary.

With less than enough undertaking work to keep him busy, Smart was finding additional work and when fighting erupted on the South Saskatchewan River, north of Saskatoon, in 1885, he bought a team and wagon and engaged to haul freight for the military forces. But the period of conflict was short and Smart's services were terminated long before he reached the scenes of rebellion.

Back in Calgary, he sold the horses and wagon and on August 24th in that year of 1885, he was one of those signing for service in Calgary's new Volunteer Hook, Ladder and Bucket Corps, thereby becoming a Charter Member of the proud force in which he was to serve at every level over the next 50 years.

James Smart appears in the records as Hose Captain in 1891, Secretary-treasurer of the Brigade in 1892 and Assistant Chief in 1897. Then, after serving under Chiefs Steve Jarrett, Frank Dick, E. R. Rogers and H. McClelland, James Smart became Chief Smart or Chief "Cappy" Smart on March 21, 1898.

Highlights were numerous in Cappy Smart's colorful career but the one that deserves first place in departmental history was the bold policy of replacing fire horses with motorized equipment. It wasn't easy. It meant breaking with tradition and resisting pres-

Chief Smart and early officers, 1902.

sures from vociferous and politically-strong horse-mens' organizations. Loyal horsemen refused to believe that mechanical power would ever displace horses in agriculture, city transport or fire fighting.

Adding to Cappy's problems was the fact that he loved horses, just as he loved dogs and all animals, wild or domestic. He was never without animal pets and some of them brought trouble. He could have horses and dogs — even a parrot — without fear of complications but when he became the possessor of a mean tempered monkey, an alligator and then a bear, troubles were compounded.

B. Newstead and parrots at fire headquarters.

Barney, the monkey, was a gift from one of Smart's friends in British Columbia. In acknowledging delivery, Cappy wrote: "the bloody bastard arrived O.K. but we had a hell of a time getting him out

Ted Knight with monkey mascot (monkey also known as Joco).

of the box. We have him installed at headquarters, chained securely, and he is beginning to get acquainted with the boys. He sits up and wonders what in hell is happening when the alarm sounds and he sees the horses running out."[1]

But Barney never became amenable and after being teased by firemen for almost a year and a half, he struck out at a small boy offering peanuts and clawed the child's face severely. Barney had to pay for his mistake and on Cappy's orders, was destroyed.

Then there was the alligator, sent with the compliments of George Fowler from Georgia. Fowler had been in Calgary to help with the installation of the first piece of motor apparatus, the 4-cylinder general purpose truck introduced in 1910.[2] It was Fowler's pleasure in meeting and knowing Cappy that led to the novel though not loveable gift.

There is no indication of the alligator disturbing the peace of the community but Cappy was not as lucky with his bear. Major, the brown bear cub brought from the mountains was a popular attraction, commonly chained to a post in front of No. 1 Fire Hall. But cubs grow up and dispositions can change. Tragedy, sad to say, struck on a Saturday afternoon in 1911 when a small girl, unattended, toddled close to the bear and was crushed and mauled by the animal. The child was rushed to hospital but died later in the day and Major promptly paid with his life.[3]

Fireman with bear cub mascot.
(Noodles the bear)

Pets of the Fire Brigade

Bud Smart and Lou Tarrant with horses.

Department Mascot.

Nig, the dog.

Cappy's associations with horses brought no heartaches except for the necessity of having to part with them and replace them with cold machines. He was the first Chief in Canada and one of the first on the continent to see the motorized apparatus as offering more efficiency, more economy and a net advantage when compared with horse-drawn equipment. The horses had to go to make way for the motors. The pioneer efforts in converting from horses to motors are recounted elsewhere.

Although he had many narrow escapes, Cappy's only serious accident occurred soon after his advocacy of a completely motorized department. He was riding in the relatively new Chief's car and speeding to a fire on November 15, 1912, when the vehicle was in collision with a street car at the intersection of 9th Avenue and 2nd Street, Southeast. The car was largely demolished and Cappy was rushed to hospital with what were soon recognized as serious injuries. He disapproved of windshields and the threat of flying glass on fire vehicles and on this occasion he was hurled through the air to strike the street car. Recovery was slow — almost two years — and it explained why he missed the biggest fire in Calgary history, the one that destroyed the Burns Abattoir in 1913.

James "Cappy" Smart, fire chief from 1898-1933.

Chief's car, 1911. McLaughlin Buick after collision with street car.

Cappy had his vices and didn't try to hide them but regardless of the counter attractions, his duty in fire prevention and control came first. He was one of the best informed students of fire fighting techniques in his time. He was one of the first to emphasize fire prevention as a fireman's duty as much as suppression. He got himself appointed as Calgary's first Fire Prevention Officer and was one of the first to advocate the office of Fire Marshal.

It was hardly surprising that Calgary people loved Cappy Smart. City fathers may have considered his dismissal on one occasion for a drinking offence but they soon discovered that public opinion would not let them do it.

Citizens knew that where they found Cappy, they would also find action and entertainment. They felt reassured when they could see and hear him at a fire, generally shouting orders through a megaphone to his men or to sidewalk spectators when they came too close for their own good. Listeners said his words seemed, at times, to be as hot as the flames he was fighting but his men knew he would never order them to take risks that he would not take.

The public loved it when Cappy would choose the notable Mother Fulham — Calgary's lady keeper of pigs — with whom to lead the Grand March at a St. Patrick's Day ball. They chuckled with delight when they heard Leishman McNeill's story of Cappy's formal presentation to visiting royalty. The Duke of York was in Calgary for a day in 1904 and Indian Chiefs from nearby reserves were invited to meet him. Dressed splendidly in their blue coats with brass buttons which had been presented by the Government of Canada at the time of Treaty negotiations, the Chiefs were presented one at a time.

Cappy, in blue uniform and brass buttons, was the next in line and was introduced with the words: "This, Your Highness, is Chief Smart." For the Duke there was but one conclusion and he was heard to whisper in an aside: "What a splendid looking Indian!"[4]

Cappy, as might have been expected, had the last word: "Yes, Your Highness, an oatmeal savage."

Throughout his 48 years as an active Calgary fire fighter, plus two years as Fire Prevention Officer to bring the total to an imposing half century, James Smart was one of the best known and influential citizens in Calgary, sharing the distinction with Paddy Nolan, James Walker, Senator James Lougheed, Bob Edwards and R. B. Bennett — all of whom were his friends. Citizens were reminded again and again at the time of his death, July 25, 1939, that they should not forget James Cappy Smart because there would be no more quite like him.

Cappy is laid to rest.

Union Cemetery, Calgary.

1. Col. Walker, 2. Tom McCauley, 3. Bill Gardner, 4. Harry, 5. Reporter Riddle, 6. The German Landscape Expert, 7. Sir Max Aiken, Major?.

[1] Smart, James, Letter to Andy Good, Summit Hotel, Crows Nest, B.C., Feb. 23, 1910. Copy of letter in Glenbow Alberta Archives, Calgary.
[2] Calgary Daily News, April 16, 1910.
[3] Albertan, May 17, 1911.
[4] McNeill, Leishman, Tales of the Old Town, p. 29. Published by Calgary Herald, 1950.

Enter The "Buzz-Wagons" — Exit The Fire Horses

Fire horses that pranced impatiently at the sound of every alarm bell were faithful and lovable but their motorized competitors were faster and, especially in idle hours, more economical. Under the circumstances, no power or sentiment on earth could halt the advance of mechanization. Calgary's Cappy Smart was one of the first to sense the change and prepare for it. Cappy's love for horses was never in doubt but for a dedicated fireman efficiency had to be of first importance and his years as Chief embraced the complete change from total dependence upon horses to the exclusive use of motorized apparatus. Calgary was said to be the first city in Canada to have a totally mechanized fire department.

Chief's horse drawn buggy.

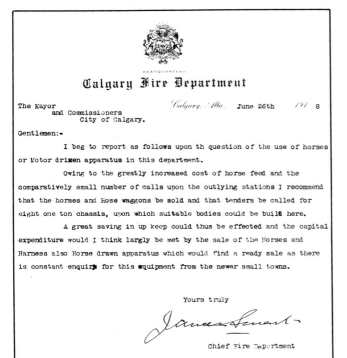

While the city in 1906 was buying a horse-drawn buggy for the needs of the Chief, — a fancy vehicle with rubber tires, a hand brake, nickel hubcaps, C.F.D. in large gold letters on the side and cost of

$225 — Smart was warning that his next request for a conveyance for the Chief would call for an automobile.

The first formal request for a motor vehicle was in the Chief's Report to Mayor and Aldermen for 1908. It had been a good year in point of fire control; a total fire loss of $67,153 on property valued at $1,188,282 was seen as reason for satisfaction but Smart wanted to make it better. He was asking for a new fire hall for the west end of the city, an extension of the alarm system by the addition of a new "six-circuit switchboard with repeater and 15 more alarm boxes," more fully-paid firemen and, revolutionary as it may have seemed, "a motor-chemical apparatus to be stationed at headquarters and used with a 'flying squadron' to serve the whole city, the same to be capable of carrying eight men, thus saving the expense of keeping a larger force of men at each substation."[1] Such a piece of apparatus, the Chief added, would substantially reduce the need for horses, being "far more economical and able to cover double the distance in half the time."

Members of the Council considered seriously.

Certain members believed it would be safer to buy another horse-drawn vehicle, perhaps the American LaFrance ladder wagon with ladders capable of extension to 65 feet, a tiller steering arrangement to help in taking long ladders around sharp turns and standing room on running boards for six or eight firemen, priced at $4,000 at the American shipping point. "Buy something like this," it was suggested, "and let another city experiment with the motor truck."

But gradually the City Commissioners came to Smart's point of view and on August 25, 1909, the Chief was making his formal and successful recommendation for the purchase of "one motor combination chemical and squad truck manufactured by the Webb Motor Fire Apparatus Co. of Indiana; the said motor is 4-cylinder, 40 horse power, air cooled with speed of 40 miles per hour and equipped with a 50-gallon chemical tank." The price was $6,000. The same requisition covered the "purchase from Obenchain and Boyer, also of Indiana, of one standard horse-drawn combination hose and chemical wagon for $1,875 and three standard hose wagons with ladders and hand extinguishers at $750." With a discount of $150 for cash, it was still a $9,975 order and by late December it had Council's approval.

The delivery of the history-making fire truck was greeted with widespread public interest. Cappy Smart was said to be looking forward to the event the way a father would await the birth of his firstborn. The talk of the town on February 10, 1910, was that the new fire engine had arrived and Smart and members of his department were so eager that they worked from 7 p.m. until 1 a.m. to unload the new pieces and bring them to headquarters.

According to the press of that date: "The New Fire Fighting Apparatus Arrived Last Night. It Is Very Swell." As the Chief told the press: "It is the best equipment of the kind that ever entered Canada. . . . I never saw apparatus that looked so substantial and, at the same time, so elegantly finished. It is finished like a grand piano. . . . The firemen are as proud of it as school boys with their first sleds."[3]

Eleven days after delivery of the new "buzz-wagon", as one editor chose to call the fire truck, it had its first real test. In responding to a call from the Clarendon Block, the "Buzz-Wagon" and its "flying squadron" were on the scene long before other vehicles arrived.[4]

With the new Webb fire truck came an expert from the factory, George Fowler, to instruct the man who had been hired as a motor mechanic in the care of the machine. The visitor was a congenial fellow and he and the Chief became instant friends. One of the Calgary experiences this man with the pleasant Georgia drawl would not forget was the loud and eloquent debate that erupted between the Fire Chief and Police Chief about speed limits. Fowler was seated beside the Calgary fireman who was learning to drive and travelling at close to 40 miles per hour which was about the vehicle's limit, when a city police officer called upon the driver to halt. The officer's accusation was of driving at roughly twice the legal speed on city streets. If it happened again, a formal charge would be laid.

Motor driven vehicle with horse drawn apparatus.

The city government had indeed passed a bylaw to allow horse-drawn fire units to exceed the general speed limit for horse vehicles but no such bylaw provided special speeding privileges for motor trucks, regardless of their purpose.

Back at headquarters, the Chief received a report of the policeman's indiscretion and "hit the ceiling" with words for which Cappy was widely known. He called Police Chief Mackie by telephone and told him much "that isn't contained in the bylaws of the City of Calgary or any other city."[5]

Chief Mackie's defence was that he had no authority to allow any automobile vehicle to exceed the city speed limit of 20 miles per hour. Smart's response to this was that the Police Chief had better act quickly to get the needed authority because any policeman who showed the bad judgment of stopping or restraining the fire truck when answering a fire call and every second might be important, was liable to be run down.

The City Commissioners, no doubt amused by this verbal "battle of the giants," took the hint and obtained hasty approval for the bylaw that would permit drivers of the "buzz-wagon" to get to a fire without needless loitering or obstruction by police officers.

Calgary's Webb fire engine became the most widely publicized thing of its kind on the continent. Enquiries concerning its performance came from far parts of United States and Canada. "How is it standing up to its work?" one writer asked. "Is it a reliable starter? How does it perform in cold weather? Would you recommend it?"

What Smart told the enquiring parties was about what he reported in a letter to the Webb Company: "I might inform you that the satisfaction received from your apparatus — received 14 months ago — is marvelous, makes horse-drawn vehicles look like a thing of the past. A big saving in maintenance, climbs grades clad with snow when the thermometer

"CALGARY FLYING SQUADRON."

Webb car, fire department's first piece of motorized equipment. "Cappy" Smart, standing, right. Crew known as "The Flying Squadron."

is registering 50 below, where horses would not go. . . . On the strength of the good work done we have just awarded your company an order for one motor hose wagon, one motor combination and one motor 75-foot aerial ladder truck."[6]

Webb aerial "gas electric", 1913.

So thoroughly convinced was Smart that in writing to the Fire Chief at Guelph, Ontario, he declared: "No more horse-drawn apparatus for me. Motors are so much quicker, can cover more ground and be economical in every way."[7]

Calgary residents who saw the first automobile on their streets in 1903 — a Stanley steamer introduced by Rancher William Cochrane — watched an automotive invasion in the next few years and now, just seven years after the coming of the Cochrane car, the Calgary car owners — 40 of them — were conducting a Saturday car parade on city thoroughfares and there at the middle of the car display, without needless modesty, was the automotive pride of the Fire Department, the first motor fire truck in this part of the West.

With the arrival of the three motor-driven pieces ordered in April, 1911 — plus a McLaughlin touring car for the Chief's special needs — the Calgary Department could boast of having the most advanced motorized fire fighting equipment in Canada, a claim that was sounded a few times when the Western Canadian Fire Chiefs Association was in convention at Calgary in July of that year, and supported by Calgary statistics in the years following.

The total fire loss for the city in 1912 was recorded as $71,737, against a risk represented by buildings and contents of $5,130,235, acknowledged as extremely low. But the most remarkable record came in 1917 when, with population of 55,000 and total fire risk placed at $5,910,825, the total fire loss was $32,333, representing a per capita loss of only 59 cents. The Chief believed it was the lowest loss figure among all North American cities.[9] Calgary's corresponding loss figure for the next year, 1918, was 85 cents, still remarkably low.

In doorway: J. Suais, S. Hughes, On apparatus: T. Inch, W. Townly, B. Fisher, Driver: R. Trapper, W. Ritchie.

Chief Smart, S. Carr, C. Romney, J. Shearer, H. Newstead, J. Fitts.

1912 Hose Wagon. In Doorway: J. Suais, S. Hughes, Driver: R. Trapper, T. Inch, W. Townly, B. Fisher, W. Ritchie on tailboard.

Cappy Smart, Julien Smart, S. Carr.

While the record in fire control was excellent, the number of traffic accidents involving the new motor fire trucks was slightly embarrassing because most of them were with city street cars, leading citizens to ask: "When are the street cars and the fire trucks going to learn to live with each other?" But without the new semaphores at important intersections it would have been worse.

By 1918 the Chief was recommending boldly that all remaining horses and horse wagons be offered for sale by auction and the returns be used to buy additional motor vehicles. To minimize the cost of the replacement program, he suggested the purchase of "eight one-ton chassis upon which bodies could be built" in the Fire Department's own shop.

"Owing to the greatly increased cost of horse feed," Smart wrote, "a great saving in upkeep would be effected and the capital expenditure would be met largely by the sale of horses and harness and horse wagons which would find a ready sale; there is constant enquiry for equipment from small towns."[10]

The recommendation was not accepted in total and the last of the horses were not sold until 1932 but when the inventory was drawn exactly 10 years after the first motor apparatus, the historic Webb all-purpose vehicle, was delivered in 1910, it was still on the Department's list but calling for retirement. It was worn out but in disappearing, it was leaving behind an imposing generation of motorized items headed by a new McLaughlin touring car which with changes would be the Chief's car, and a Chevrolet roadster for the Assistant Chief. There were a rebuilt Fiat emergency unit, a rebuilt Boyd for salvage operations after fires, two new Nash vehicles for carrying hose, a Willys-Overland alarm car, six Webbs serving various purposes, a Kissell conversion to a hose truck, a Winston, a Ford, a Rocket Schneider, the old McLaughlin that had been the Chief's first car, the venerable Webb all-purpose "buzz-wagon" which was officially retired on the first day of September, 1920, and the new Pride of the Department, a long-bodied Webb aerial.[11] It was a startling change for a single decade.

Calgary Motor Fire Apparatus.

Calgary Fire Department vehicles and personnel, 1913-14. L-R: No. 2 Service Truck: C. Crum, T. Inch, J. Connacher, D. Sullivan. Salvage Truck: A. Barker, N. McLaughlin, T. Hughes, H. Fisher, P. Corrigan. Turrett Hose Truck: P. Simmons, A. Crocker, S. Gillespie, C. Burns, E. Burton. Hose Wagon: R. Chambers, E. Thompson, A. Cole. Chemical and Hose: R. Trapper, J. Suais, A. Newton, P. Smith. No. 1 Pump: W. Hughes, H. Wilson, B. Main, P. Sampson, R. Taylor. No. 2 Pump: E. Radshaw, A. Gibbons, J. Richardson. Aerial Ladder: W. Ritchie, W. New, C. Romney, E. Dreyfus, H. Newstead. Assistant Chief's Car: A. Carr, L. Tarrant. Chief's Car: James Smart, G. Bartlett.

Webb Gas Electric Aerial, 1913. Driver: ?. Back: P. Corrigan, S. Carr, B. Taylor, W. Townley. Front: ?, A. Simmons, A. McLaughlin, W. Ritchie.

Left: Studebaker Pump Engine. Right: Studebaker Hose and Chemical Engine.

[1] Smart, James, Annual Report to Mayor and Aldermen, City of Calgary, Dec. 31, 1908.
[2] Albertan, Feb. 10, 1910.
[3] Albertan, Feb. 10, 1910.
[4] Albertan, Feb. 21, 1910.
[5] Calgary Daily News, March 10, 1910.
[6] Smart, James, Letter to O. S. Doolittle, Webb Motor Fire Apparatus Co., St. Louis, Missouri, April 26, 1911 (Copy of letter at Glenbow Archives).
[7] Smart, James, Letter to Fire Chief, Guelph, Ont. Feb. 22, 1910 (Glenbow Archives).
[8] Calgary Daily Herald, March 12, 1910.
[9] Smart, James, Annual Report of Chief of Fire Department, Calgary, Dec. 31, 1917.
[10] Smart, James, Letter to Mayor and Commissioners, City of Calgary, June 26, 1918.
[11] Smart, James, Annual Report, Calgary Fire Department, Dec. 31, 1920.

Bigger And Better Machines

The motor equipment that made the Calgary Fire Department a Canadian leader in 1920 was, by 1928, showing wear and obsolescence. Replacements during the years of post-war slump had been avoided and the Fire Chief and his officers were calling as loudly as they dared for new and better equipment.

The Mayor and members of the city council may have been sympathetic but their political savvy made them hesitant and ruled finally to let the taxpayers make the decision. A plebicite in December, 1928, would give the voters a chance to approve or disapprove a spending appropriation of $50,000 to upgrade the city's firefighting equipment. The outcome may have brought surprise to the elected officials but the balloting citizens were emphatic; 3,692 favored the expenditure and 1,582 were opposed.

The Fire Chief and his colleagues knew exactly what was needed and being well aware that fire will not wait for equipment or faltering politicians, they urged immediate action. The purchases in 1929 included a six-cylinder Nash car for the use of the Chief, a Bickle hose truck, a Bickle salvage and emergency truck, a Bickle pumper and hose truck and what was regarded as "the last word" in firefighting appliances, the German made Magirus, an aerial ladder truck with an 85-foot reach toward the sky and offering opportunity for "water tower" fighting of fires.[1] This wonder piece was one of the first three of its kind in Canada.

Margirus Aerial (Maggie).

1932 line-up.

37

Margirus aerial, 1946 group.

The big and costly Margirus to be based at No. I fire hall, took almost half of the $50,000 appropriation but remained in service for many years and according to Joe Fitts who was responsible for keeping it in good running order, proved to be an excellent investment.

To match the superiority of the imported ladder truck, Calgary needed something similarly outstanding in a pumper but had to wait a few years for it. The big and powerful American La France pumper ordered in June, 1942 and delivered in the following March, came at a cost of $12,000 and with the reputation of being one of the best available on the world market. A pumper capable of sustaining three high-pressure streams and throwing 600 gallons of water per minute would have few rivals at that time.

The new pumper was seen as a beauty and a wonder but Calgary affection was still slanted toward the Magirus, even though it was growing old. The "Maggie," as it was known, served the city both long and well but by 1948 when it was in its 20th year and showing signs of disorder and fatigue, the time had come for a replacement presenting fewer problems in obtaining repairs. But Calgarians with sentiment for aging and faithful servants and fire trucks were happy to hear that "Maggie" would be retained as a "spare rig" while its place on the front line of defence would be taken by a new mistress of the fire fleet. The new one would be another handsome aerial ladder truck, this time a Bickle-Seagrave for which the city was paying $31,750.

S. Carr, J. McKinnon, H. Glover, H. Darling, J. MacDonald, B. Hill, J. Fitts, D. Finlayson.

Enhancing its fame, the new truck came to Calgary by way of Lethbridge where it was detained for a few days for display and a bit of Calgary boasting at the convention of Canadian Fire Chiefs.

Like its predecessor, the Bickle-Seagrave had ladders capable of extension to 85 feet. One of the latter's innovations, however, was something called an "evacuator," a long bag-like creation that could be used as an emergency fire escape from high levels. The trapped person entering the canvas chute at the seventh or eighth floor of a burning building could slide quickly but not too quickly to safety at the ground level.

May 1, 1946 Group. Front Row, L-R: S. Brooks, J. Taylor, N. Strang, C. Biggs, C. Baillod, R. Sprouse, A. Sanofsky, R. Harper, W. Goodkey, A. Stuggert. Second Row: M. Kingston, T. Davidson, A. Barclay, G. Fisher, L. Collins, W. Cowan, P. Brooks, J. Fitts, J. Leinweber, L. Maley, R. Cundy, C. Davey, B. Steer, H. Tucker. Third Row: L. Broomfield, J. Huntley, G. Waslenchuk, W. Hamilton, E. Smart, M. Krasnow, K. Moody, W. Dalgetty, J. Monaghan, E. Reynolds, H. Wright, J. Kelly. Fourth Row: J. Robertson, F. Archer, D. Jackson, A. Prichard, A. Wright, H. Bolinski, J. Carrington, V. Kimmel, J. Bailey, M. Geddes, J. Johnson, A. Cassidy, E. Penny, R. Romney, L. Sexsmith, A. Flaig, M. Flowler.

1935 ladder service truck.

1946 Bickle-Seagrave Emergency.

Division Chief Joe Parish.

Line-up in early 1950's.

Advancing Through the Years

No. 5 Emergency.

No. 5 Emergency Demonstration.

1951 Bickle pumper.

At about this time, also, Calgary people were seeing the construction of a new facility for its complex fire alarm system. Early in 1950 the old alarm room at No. I fire hall was being abandoned in favor of the new centre built for the purpose at Rotary Park on the north side of the Bow. It would mark the completion of a $250,000 renovation and reconstruction of the entire system. Modern alarm boxes were installed and over 19 miles of new cables were laid to replace the underground lines laid when the system was created. Although the new system would be more complex by far, its operation would remain simple and efficiency in receiving and dispatching calls would be high.

Due to excessive false alarms, fire alarm boxes were removed from the streets in 1978.

Alarm Room, 1950.

Alarm Room, 1984.

Then came the age of computers when mechanical and electrical "hired men" and "hired women" began the performance of unbelievable services in the area of technology. By 1983 it was apparent that the already complex fire alarm system would be one of the next to be computerized.

Firefighting apparatus like the Magirus ladder truck and the American La France pumper were looked upon as marvels in their time but the big and powerful firefighting vehicles lined up for public display during Fire Prevention week in 1983, would scarcely pass for members of the same mechanical "species." In size, adaptability, shape and cost, the changes in a few years were almost as striking as the color change from fire engine red to fire engine yellow or more correctly lime green on C.F.D. vehicles.

1948 Bickle Seagrave 85 foot aerial (Silver Bell).

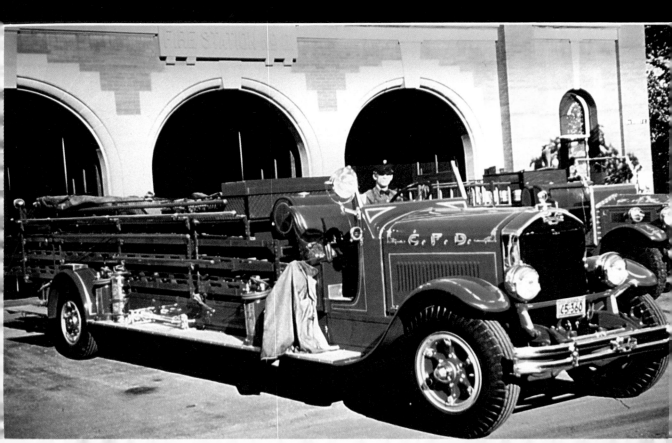

Display of Fire Apparatus at Stampede Corral.

Silver bell Aerial, 1948 Bickle-Seagrave.

No. 12 Fire Station, 17th Avenue and 37th Street S.E.

Downtown parade.

No. 13 Station apparatus.

R-81 and R-33 Airport Apparatus.

Standby Equipment at Exhibition Grounds.

Number 1 Station, 1960's.

Standby at Airport.

Airport Unit No. 1, 1962 (Walter Kruschel).

First Lime Green Apparatus appeared in 1976.

No. 4 Station (Squad Pumper)

No. 1 Rescue and Jet Boat; no. 1 Pump.

100′ Aerial at Drill School.

Looking down from 100′ Aerial.

No. 16 station squad pump and equipment.

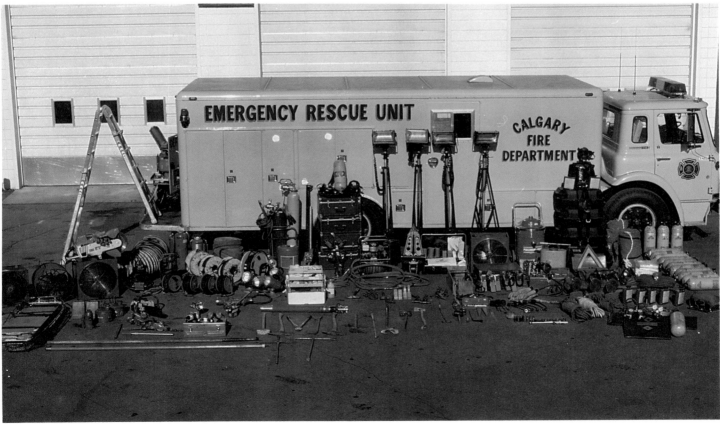

No. 16 station emergency and equipment.

What a difference 50 years can make in a department working for ever increasing effectiveness in fire control! The Fire Department that listed 20 motor vehicles in 1932 when the last of the fire horses were retired, had 140 vehicles of more costly and specialized kind and a multi-million dollar inventory in 1983. The dollar figure was the price that had to be paid for the kind of highly efficient firefighting service that people wanted.

When the clean and beautiful and useful firefighting machines were out for public inspection in the latter year, the popularity winner if a poll had been taken, would have been the half-million dollar aerial ladder truck from No. 2 fire hall known as the Firebird. What it would do was more impressive even than its massive appearance. The Firebird was the machine that would project working firemen skyward 150 feet, "half way to Heaven" as one of its attendants observed. The runners-up in such a poll were likely to be the big International-Superior pumper with replacement cost of about $100,000 and the Scott-Thibault aerial, a $150,000 unit, both from No. 1 Fire Hall.

No. 2 station Firebird.

Firebird domination among the Department's vehicles was rather like that of Dinny the Brontosaurus dinosaur among the models of ancient reptiles at Calgary's St. George's Island Park. This undisputed departmental showpiece was described as a California construction of a telescoping-articulating boom on a Hendrickson custom chassis. Under its hood was a 350 horse power, 8-cylinder V-type motor and when it was bought in 1976, it was the only one of its size and kind in Canada. When carrying a full compliment of supplies, it was said to weigh 33 tons. William Weisenburger who had a prominent part in the production of this book, was among the first to drive and operate the mechanical giant, having taken a special two-months course as preparation.

Any aerial platform apparatus that will allow firemen to fight fires from 150 feet in the air and rescue trapped victims from ninth and tenth floors of burning buildings, demands unusual skill and precaution on the part of operators. As all individuals who have had the experience of being on that platform when extended to its maximum height in the air will appreciate, the effect of even a slight wind or list for any reason, must mean hazard, hence the extreme importance of having the truck meticulously level and positively firm on its supports.

Fire Bird in Action

That high-pressure pumper rating high in public interest and esteem in 1983 would have filled Cappy Smart with amazement if he could have seen it. In being able to bring eight powerful streams of water against a fire, it would be far ahead of the best of which Smart ever dreamed.

Viewers at the Fire Prevention week display in 1983 were known to comment: "Yes, it cost a lot of money but how many big fires does a high-priced pumper have to check and choke to justify its cost?" However members of the public may answer, firemen have given it as their opinion that this big, $100,000 unit weighing roughly 32,000 pounds when speeding to a fire, has saved enough for home and business owners to pay for itself many times.

With multiple streams of water, high pressure and good volume, it is at once relatively easy to gain control of fire. Water at the hydrant is under pressure of about 75 pounds but after passing through the big pumper the pressure is up to some 300 pounds and can be thrown at a fire at the rate of 1750 gallons per minute; that is the rated delivery of the water but men who have operated the pumper say the volume can be increased to a maximum of 2350 gallons.

Fire Boss.

M.O.T. Fire Boss units in action at airport.

Super pump.

Still more specialized was an apparatus like the Fire Boss with one big tank of dry chemicals and one of foam, especially effective in combatting gasoline fires. Bigger units of the kind might have been seen at the International Airport where the Calgary Fire Department assumed responsibility for fire control in the years of the older McCall Field and continued to furnish the services when the Calgary International Airport evolved. With their own Fire Hall and their own unique problems, the airport firefighters have indeed enjoyed distinction as well as responsibility.

If someone like Cappy Smart could return for a visit at the new No. 1 Fire Hall, he would point to many other firefighting wonders on wheels, asking again and again: "What's this?" One of the objects would be an auxiliary electric power unit, a mobile piece of apparatus offering insurance against complete power failure in case of some major disaster, enough to keep the essential services in operation.

And for the person interested in water safety and rescue, the same No. 1 Fire Hall could show advanced equipment like the simple looking gadget called a "res-q-dek". Its appearance would be enough to make any visitor want to stop to ask questions. If this rescue unit had a pedigree, the observer could be excused for speculating about one parent being an airplane and the other a common rubber raft. With two big inflated floats to give suspension, the craft is furnished with a 25 horse power outboard motor, and the stability to manoeuver in the dangerous waters of the dreaded weir. (The weir being a dam across the Bow River in East Calgary which diverts water for irrigation to Southern Alberta and which has earned the unenviable name of "The Drowning Machine".)

Also housed at No. 1 is the patrol and rescue jet boat, a new 22 foot aluminum river boat powered by a 454 cu. in. Mercury inboard and a Hamilton Jet Drive. Designed especially for river work, it is capable of skimming over the river in only nine (9) inches of water at speeds up to 35 m.p.h. It replaces the 24 foot patrol boat which has been sent to cover the three man-made lakes in south Calgary, and was donated by the Alberta Government to the Department.

Mobile electric generator.

Res-q-dek.

Jet boat 806.

Aquatics training exercise in Bow River, 1984.

For further information with respect to this chapter, see Appendix C, Page 190.

[1] Smart, James, Annual Report to Mayor and Aldermen, City of Calgary, Dec. 31, 1908.
[2] Albertan, Feb. 10, 1910.
[3] Albertan, Feb. 10, 1910.
[4] Albertan Feb. 21, 1910.
[5] Calgary Daily News, March 10, 1910.
[6] Smart, James, Letter to O. S. Doolittle, Webb Motor Fire Apparatus Co., St. Louis, Missouri, April 26, 1911 (Copy of letter at Glenbow Archives).
[7] Smart, James, Letter to Fire Chief, Guelph, Ont. Feb. 22, 1910 (Glenbow Archives).
[8] Calgary Daily Herald, March 12, 1910.
[9] Smart, James, Annual Report of Chief of Fire Department, Calgary, Dec. 31, 1917.
[10] Smart, James, Letter to Mayor and Commissioners, City of Calgary, June 26, 1918.
[11] Smart, James, Annual Report, Calgary Fire Department, Dec. 31, 1920.
[12] Calgary Fire Department Annual Report, 1930.

No. 17 Fire Station and Apparatus.

No. 16 Fire Station Aerial Apparatus.

"An Ounce Of Prevention . . ."

Cappy Smart was not the first to say that "an ounce of prevention is worth more than a pound of cure," but he echoed it and was one of the first to entrench the idea in the code of firefighters.

Fire prevention was an area in which he was an unquestioned pioneer. Over the years he may have been given credits he did not deserve and been blamed for sins he did not commit but nobody could deny his stubborn zeal for the crucial importance of reaching a fire quickly and overwhelming it before it had time to establish itself. And better still, he argued long before administrations were ready to act, the best efforts should be made to remove the conditions allowing fires to start.

Even in 1912, the Chief was using his annual report to tell the Mayor and aldermen that the time had come for the appointment of a fire prevention officer to work under him in locating and removing the causes of fire. The officer would make inspections, with the purpose of removing the hazards and he would methodically study the causes of fires as they occured. Hopefully, his labors would generate a new interest in striking at fires before they started.

During the year in question, according to the annual report, 38 Calgary fires were believed to have started from defective chimneys, 31 from hot ashes,

31 were prairie fires, 21 resulted from improperly supervised burning of rubbish and 10 from children playing with matches. The point should have been clear that all these fires were preventable.[1]

In the next year, 1913, the message was repeated even more clearly: "I strongly recommend the immediate appointment of a Fire Marshal or inspector whose duties shall be the inspection of all fire escapes, furnaces, fire places, theatres, etc., and everything pertaining to fire risk and safety. His duties would include the investigation of the causes of fires."[2]

The same note was sounded year after year in Smart's annual reports but the administration seemed to be satisfied in having formally named the Chief as a Fire Inspector which meant nothing more than confirming his authority for what he had been doing without special authorization. Readers of the pioneer newspapers might note under date of May 10, 1911, that the Fire Chief was making a general inspection of all garages in the city.[3]

From 1921 Smart was asking with almost monotonous regularity for a Fire Prevention Bureau rather than a Fire Marshal but still not receiving much encouragement. This more pretentious objective was not realized for 30 years and Smart, at the time of his retirement in 1933, acknowledged that one of his few disappointments was in coming to the end of his active career before his city gained the benefits of such a Bureau.

It wasn't the first good idea that was slow in being adopted and implemented but a Calgary Fire Prevention Bureau did become a reality on May 15, 1951, twelve years after Cappy Smart's death prevented him from seeing it.

Ironically, the ultimate adoption of the Fire Prevention Bureau idea came as a result of a visit from Fire Chief G. G. Burnett of Ottawa, acting as a consultant to make an outsider's assessment of ways to improve fire protection in Calgary. The proposal to bring the eastern stranger as an adviser generated some strong criticism from within the Department. The critics seemed to be vindicated when it was noted that many of the visitor's proposals had been made at various times and fallen upon deaf ears. It was noted also that if Chief Cappy Smart was still around to see his city buying and promptly adopting the Prevention Bureau idea with which he had labored without much satisfaction for decades, his wrath would have been hot enough to start a spontaneous combustion fire in his section of the city.

"The Calgary Fire Department today put into operation its first Fire Prevention Bureau, staffed with five men who will conduct regular inspections of all major buildings and dwellings in the city," the press reported on May 15, 1951.[4]

Lew Marks Certificate of Merit for Fire Prevention: Fire Chief Barney Lemieux.

"The Bureau has long been sought by the Fire Department as a means of eliminating many fire hazards as yet undiscovered," the news report stated. "The prevention service is under the direction of Chief Fire Prevention officer, D. J. McDougall and his assistants are Logan Brown, Lew Marks, Rupert Binnion and Myles Kingston. All have served at least five years with the Calgary department."

Each of these officers was being assigned the responsibility for the inspection of certain classes of buildings; one man would maintain a watch upon theatres, hotels and apartment blocks, another would be expected to check hospitals and institutional homes and the others would have their categories, schools in one case, restaurants and dance halls in another.

Nor would the new concept be limited to inspections, not by any means. Educational programs with lectures at schools and community gatherings, and fire drills at hospitals, industrial plants and where fire dangers were likely to lurk.

The new branch was still part of the Fire Department and would conduct its work under complete liaison with the departmental Chief and fire station Captains.

In the years that followed, the Calgary Fire Prevention Bureau gained headlines by its bold and numerous innovations. Men in the service seized every opportunity to tell school classes about the seriousness of fire dangers and what citizens — young and old — can do to minimize the risks; they directed fire alarm drills at schools, hospitals, factories and wherever people were working in large numbers and thereby increasing risks.

Calgarians, it seemed, responded to become almost instantly more conscious of fire hazards and, regardless of how it could be explained, the city in the very next year, 1952, won the second highest award for fire prevention in Canadian cities with population in excess of 100,000; and in 1954, the same city won the highest award in the same category, a success that was repeated in 1968.

As the educational program continued, Calgary citizens saw a Fire Prevention parade — the first — in 1956. In the next year they had opportunity to witness the first Industrial Fire Prevention course of instruction and public interest was such that the number of applications exceeded the 200 who could be accommodated and some of the candidates had to be turned away.

Fire Prevention Parade.

There would be no relaxation of effort in preventing fires but citizens and servants of the Bureau could, in 1959, take satisfaction in the knowledge that Calgary was still the "most fire-safe city in Canada." In the words of the press of that time: "No other major metropolitan centre can claim a record close to that of Calgary in the past decade, either in fatalities, injuries or property damage resulting from fires. The Calgary Fire Department has managed to hold total losses below $1,000,000 in eight of the past 10 years and the record of the remaining two years was ruined only by single fires."[5]

For a city with population of 219,000 and sprawled over 75 square miles, it was the best of reason for pride.

Scarcely surprising, the Fire College idea gained favor. Suggested by Calgary Chief Barney Lemieux, in the course of a Fire Chiefs convention at Banff in 1957, its purpose was, obviously, to bring together new techniques and old ones in dealing with fires. Alberta was quick to adopt the college principle and attendance at college courses soared. At least a few of the 600 delegates from United States, United Kingdom and Canada attending the convention of the Canadian Association of Fire Chiefs meeting at the Palliser Hotel in Calgary in September 1960, confessed that they came quite largely to gain information about the new Fire College.

Fire Prevention Chief, Douglas J. McDougall — son of the widely known missionary of frontier years, Rev. John McDougall, retired after 38 years of Fire

I. Beecher, B. Thompson, R. Harper, J. Jack.

Department service at the end of 1959 and was succeeded in the office by Lew Marks who joined the Department in 1936 and was one of the original members of the Fire Prevention Bureau. The new Fire Marshal reminded the public that prevention of fires was still his primary purpose and he and his staff would continue to pursue that end by all known techniques and some new ones. Building inspections would occupy most of the time of his Bureau personnel and himself but as in the past, his department would diversify its efforts to get everybody working for prevention. In the Bureau's most recent year, he noted, fires investigated by his staff had numbered 528, to say nothing of lectures, demonstrations and the 176,000 items of literature that had been distributed.

Still more impressive was Marks' summary of the first 11 years of the Fire Prevention Bureau, presented in 1962. For this total period, members of the Bureau had made 119,428 building inspections, given 2,861 safety lectures, conducted 6,047 fire drills and removed or corrected 6,149 hazardous situations in Calgary buildings, "all in an effort to save lives and property."[6]

Chief Shelley at F.P.B. Demonstration.

Logan Brown Fire Extinguisher Practical Demonstration.

F. Parker demonstrating gasoline detector.

Lew Marks at retirement in 1970 was succeeded as Fire Marshal by Rupert Binnion and the latter in 1976 by Myles Kingston who became the fourth Fire Marshal to be named from the original members of the Fire Prevention Bureau of 1951. Retirement for Mr. Kingston came in 1979, after 33 years of active association with the C.F.D., and he was followed by C. G. Stuart as Calgary's fifth Fire Marshal.

First CFD/Police arson team H. Anderson and B. Davidson. B. Davidson died in the line of police duty, December 20, 1974.

S. MacKenzie demonstrating in-house fire phone.

Joe Lewko informing police constable of fire details.

Fire Prevention

Could Have
Prevented
Many of
These Scenes

One of the recent Fire Marshals observed that 33 years after the Fire Prevention Bureau was started, it has no less to do than when it began. "It has a job that never ends and never diminishes in importance," he said. He pointed at the Bureau's big annual week-long displays and shows at North Hill and Chinook shopping centres in Calgary, marking Fire Prevention Week. It was his message that they are considered as important to public understanding as at any time since they were inaugurated in 1951 and the response from men, women and children proves the interest is mutual.

It was all in the good name of fire protection.

[1] Smart, James, Annual Report of Calgary Fire Department to Mayor and aldermen, 1912.
[2] Smart, James, Annual Report, 1913.
[3] Calgary News Telegram, May 10, 1911.
[4] Calgary Herald, May 15, 1951.
[5] Calgary Herald, June 20, 1959.
[6] Calgary Herald, Aug. 18, 1962.
[7] Calgary Herald, July 20, 1964.

Percy Baker, Les McMillan.

Community Display.

Community Display.

John Johnston

F.P.B. Bureau, 1976.

Debbie Balaux, Jim Duffin.

Fire Prevention Helpers

Rescue And Safety

Community firemen, from the earliest years, were expected to be men of many parts, ready and able to serve the public in the face of disaster from fire to flood. When Calgary residents in 1897 caught a vision of serious flood trouble, they turned to men of the volunteer Fire Brigade, as instinctively as a hungry robin looks for worms.

A three-inch rain coinciding with the seasonal surge of melt-water from the mountains, drove the river level to its highest point in the memory of settlers, making officers of the North West Mounted Police wonder if the choice of site for a fort at the confluence of the two foothill and mountain streams was a mistake.

Langevin bridge.

The Bow overflowed its banks to give the impression of a lake more than a river. Floods covered the area that became Sunnyside and the menacing water reached as far as Sixth Avenue on the south side. Rail grades were washed out and train service was disrupted with westbound trains terminating temporarily at Calgary and eastbound trains at Banff. Sixty families had to be evacuated and a few houses floated away. Luckily, only one life was lost but damage would have been much heavier if it had not been for firemen seen wading in hip-deep water, with no better footwear than knee-high rubber boots.

Among the casualties was the Bow Marsh bridge at present day Tenth Street. H. B. Wilson whose connection with the C.F.D. began in 1889, the year he came to Calgary from his home in Ontario, was an eyewitness and told his story. As a fireman, he had been assigned the duties of night watchman at the bridge and at 5 a.m., after walking across the structure and finding it trembling from the turbulance of the water, he paused to speak to a workman at Eau Claire Lumber.

"Look!" exclaimed the workman. "There goes our bridge." Sure enough, the bridge over which Fireman Wilson had just walked, was floating past, riding the river like a break-away raft — until it struck the Langevin Bridge and crumpled like an apple barrel.

A Calgary Fire Department Souvenir Booklet published in 1904 reported briefly: "A serious flood of the Bow River occurred [in 1897]. The Brigade was called out and did heroic work rescuing residents on the water front. They were voted $75 for services."[1]

But as Calgary firemen were soon to discover, the tasks of rescue could appear in a thousand forms. It could be the family cat that foolishly pursued a sparrow to the rooftop and didn't know how to get down. It might be the horse that stumbled into the unguarded sewer excavation on Stephen Avenue and was in hopeless trouble until two resourceful firemen came with shovels and proceeded to fill the trench. As the clay was returned to the hole, the horse stood higher on the fill and was finally able to walk out unharmed.

More serious, however, was the position of the horse that tried to cross the irrigation canal and Ogden Road on the Canadian National Railway bridge and made the misstep that allowed all four feet to pass through between the ties, leaving the animal resting on its belly, dangling its legs, and completely stranded.

Train movements in the region were halted and members of the Fire Brigade, including Division Chief C. F. Hopkinson, were summoned. A railroad representative arrived and suggested shooting the horse and removing the body in pieces. This proposal, however, was inconsistent with the firemens' idea of rescue and was rejected forthwith. Instead, the railway man was told that if he wanted to be useful he could find and deliver a couple of grain car doors.

By the time the doors were delivered, the firemen had fixed a block and tackle to the metal superstructure of the bridge. An anesthetic was administered to keep the horse from struggling and injuring itself.

When all was ready for the test, the horse was raised clear of the tracks and the grain car doors were placed across the tracks. The anesthetized horse was lowered to rest on the doors and then, by means of ropes, the doors were slid along the tracks to the end of the bridge, then across a ditch to a point where the animal could be passed under a barbed wire fence to the pasture where a band of horses stood as if to welcome their friend in misadventure back into the fold.

"Before we left," said Division Chief Hopkinson, "the horse was on its feet, looking as though it had a hard night with a bottle."[2]

High on the list of unusual C.F.D. emergencies was the one that found firemen co-operating with City Police in capturing a suspected murderer who, with gun and plenty of ammunition, barricaded himself in the cellar of an abandoned grocery store in Calgary's Tuxedo Park District in 1914.

Jack Wilson, chief clerk at the Canada Cement Company plant at Exshaw had been robbed and murdered a week earlier. A three-man gang was suspected. Two of the accused were arrested near Banff and when the third was traced to Calgary and to the abandoned store, a police posse headed by Chief Cuddy rushed to the 27th Avenue, N.E. building with small dug-out cellar. One of the police officers, speaking Russian, called to the suspect to surrender. There was no response and rather than invite a needless gun battle, the Fire Department was asked for help.

Two horse-drawn hose wagons and a crew headed by Assistant Fire Chief Carr — later Chief Carr — rushed from the Crescent Heights station to the scene of seige and a hose connection made with a nearby hydrant. The technique then followed resembled that of many farm boys who caught gophers by pouring water down their burrows and, thereby, drowning them out.

At Tuxedo Park, the trap door in the floor was raised just enough to admit a nozzle and the water was turned on. It took only a few minutes to fill the small dugout and when the water was almost reaching the floor, a rapping was heard above one corner of the excavation. A voice was heard: "I give up." A fireman's axe was used to cut a hole in the floor at the point of the rapping. The suspect, dripping wet, surrendered his revolver and then allowed himself to be drawn through the hole to be arrested.[3]

As commonly used, the terms "emergency" and "rescue" signify trouble, much like the frightening shout of "fire." The victims need help and friends — need them in a hurry. The circumstances producing emergencies, being unpredictable, are generally beyond planned protection. A citizen could take all the possible precautions against fire and drowning

66

and then be caught in a blizzard or struck down by an angry herd bull or drunken driver. But such uncertainty concerning dangers was just one more reason for a versatile rescue squad, as the C.F.D. and City of Calgary concluded.

A bright new day for rescue and safety in Calgary dawned near the end of 1951 when a shining red rescue truck, fully equipped with lifesaving aids was presented to the city by the Associated Canadian Travellers. The first person to dream realistically about such a vehicle was William A. Phillips who came from his native Scotland as a baby of seven months and became a noted athlete and athletic trainer. He seemed to be preordained to be a fireman with a special flare for rescue and safety. Often he would jog home from school so that he might have extra time in which to run errands for firemen at Number 1 Fire Hall. On one of his boyhood visits at the Fire Hall, he was whisked away to the classroom where the firefighters were receiving instructions in first aid; they wanted the boy to serve as a subject for their practice efforts. Thereafter he was frequently a live model for first aid classes and he was learning as he served. His only worry was that an alarm bell would sound at a moment when he was thoroughly bandaged and the firemen would depart quickly, leaving him in shackles of bandages.

He began active studies with St. John Ambulance when he was 18 years old in 1930, the beginning of an association of more than 50 years. It was one aspect of his education he would turn to particularly good purpose. But not sure if his first choice of vocation was in police work or firefighting, he applied for work to both departments in Calgary and because an acceptance came through from the Fire Department first, he became a firefighter beginning on November 1, 1936.

In his enthusiasm for rescue and safety, Phillips told friends in the Associated Canadian Travellers that a gift of a properly equipped rescue truck for use across the city would be a handsome gesture and probably the means of saving many lives. The Travellers took the hint and authorized Phillips to select a truck and equipment up to $7,900 in cost. One of the most up-to-date trucks of its kind at that time was created and presented to the city.

That original red truck dedicated to rescue and safety carried the newest kinds of stretchers, emergency cutting equipment for use in freeing people trapped in wreckage, three very modern self contained breathing apparatus, a special gun for shooting a lifeline to somebody in trouble, hydraulic jacks, floodlamps, lifejackets, a pneolator, the latest aid in restoring breathing following asphyxiation and first aid supplies.

The new truck, Phillips said, was not intended to take the place of an ambulance but there would be many instances as in cases of asphyxiation and accident when it would fill a distinct need. That red truck did indeed serve a special purpose until 1963 when it was showing its age and was replaced by a white one, somewhat bigger and fitted with newer facilities.

In the meantime, Phillips was performing and teaching more effective methods of artificial respiration. With advice from Dr. L. S. Mackid and certain other doctors, he was pioneering with the direct mouth-to-mouth technique, closed chest cardiac massage and obtaining great encouragement. After the city took over all ambulance services in 1971, Phillips became Division Chief for such.

W. A. Phillips with first CFD rescue car.

With the Department's traditional role in rescue, it seemed logical that it could and should be made responsible for ambulance services in the City. Up to 1970 private operators furnished emergency transportation of sick and injured people, mainly to hospital, but following a period of unrest among ambulance workers and then a strike in 1970, there were strong recommendations that the ambulance service be taken over by the City and placed with the Fire Department. The City Council approved and the Ambulance Division of the Calgary Fire Department came into existence early in 1971, continuing for the next thirteen years. Then after more debate, the City Council in 1983 moved to allow the separation of the City's Ambulance services from the Calgary Fire Department.

Then another rescue innovation. This time it was in water safety and it was announced in October, 1958, that 24 Calgary firefighters were embarking upon a course in skin diving. Calgary would be the first city in the West and the second in Canada to have a crew of aquatics in the Fire Department.[4]

As boating and other water sports grew in favor, dangers increased and a bigger stock of rescue boats was needed. Craft with more manoeuvrability, more speed and more equipment were added until the C.F.D. officials were boasting that they had the best trained and furnished rescue teams in Canada. By 1973 Fire Chief Derek Jackson was saying confidently that this Department was in a position to assume control of any disaster situation in the area. "We are ready," he said.

After another decade, the Department had five rescue trucks, all with more sophisticated aids for use in emergencies, such things as heavy duty cutting tools known as "jaws of life," and powered saws capable of cutting quickly through heavy iron doors and concrete walls. Other citizens were repeating: "Our firemen are ready."

[1] Historic and Illustrated Souvenir of Calgary Fire Department, p. 37, 1904.
[2] Hopkinson, C. F., The Rescue of a Horse, manuscript loaned to author, Jan., 1983.
[3] Calgary Herald, June 3, 1914.
[4] Calgary Herald, Oct. 6, 1958.

Rescue demonstration. Emergency rescue unit and equipment.

"Jaws of life" Hurst power tool.

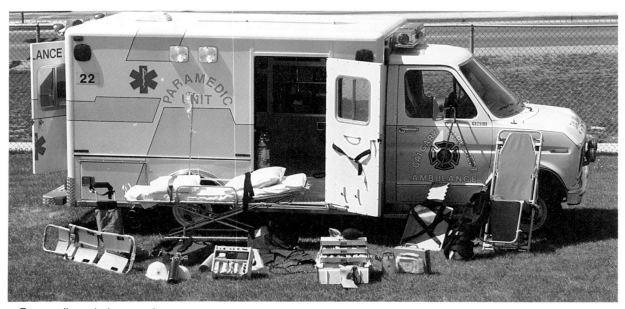

Paramedic ambulance unit.

River ice rescue practice.

Helicopter river rescue practice.

Chained buoys installed by C.F.D. at Bow River weir.

River patrol mall demonstration (G. Borkristl).

Sailboat rescue training at Glenmore.

Water rescue and CPR practice.

Rescue boat and helicopter exercise.

Aquatics rescue course safety demonstration (what not to do).

Simulated aircraft rescue in Bow River, Spring, 1984.

Their "Most Memorable" Fires

No big community escapes big fires. If in doubt, ask the retired fireman.

Just as every town or city has experienced certain fires that were bigger, more costly and more persistent than others, so every older firefighter can recall ones that stand out prominently in memory and about which he is ready to talk.

When the elder firemen from C.F.D. service were presented, in 1983, with the question: "Which fires in your years as a fireman linger as the most memorable?" the replies came readily and the ones mentioned most frequently were: the Empire hotel fire on January 18, 1920; the Wales hotel and annex fire on October 1, 1941; the Union Packing Company plant at Nose Creek, December 29, 1948; the No. 5 Hangar at the Municipal Airport, December 6, 1954; the Marshall Wells building, 1955; the Cameron Block, November 29, 1961; and the Glencoe Club fire on January 9, 1962.

Central Methodist Church, 7th Avenue and 1st Street S.W., February 29, 1916.

Capitol Barber Shop, 100 Block, 8th Avenue S.E. December 6, 1949.

Only one of the Calgary pensioners consulted in 1983 could speak as an on-the-spot viewer at fires as early as 1913 when the Burns Packing Company plant in Calgary was destroyed. That one was Syd Hughes who joined the Calgary Fire Brigade in 1914 — three years after coming from London England — and, hence, in watching the big Burns fire in 1913, he was doing it as an interested citizen rather than a fireman. But the fact remained that he saw it and had no hesitation in declaring it the most memorable of the hundreds of fires he witnessed in a long career.

Empire Hotel, 118-9th Avenue S.E., January 18, 1920.

CNR Express Station, 18th Avenue and Centre Street S.W., 1920.

Parish and Heimbecker Elevator, 11th Avenue and 11th Street S.E., June 21, 1963.

Marshall Wells Ltd., 118-11 Ave. S.E., April 6, 1955.

Glencoe Club, 29th Avenue and 6th Street S.W., January 9, 1962.

McArthur Furniture/Gainers Meats, 11th Avenue and 5th Street S.W., March 6, 1954.

Osbornes, 112-8th Avenue S.W., March 20, 1966.

McArthur Furniture, 235-10th Ave. S.W., April 3, 1972.

Chinatown fire, 10th Avenue and 1st Street S.E., October, 1912.

Woolworth's fire, 200 Block, 8th Avenue S.W., November 19, 1921.

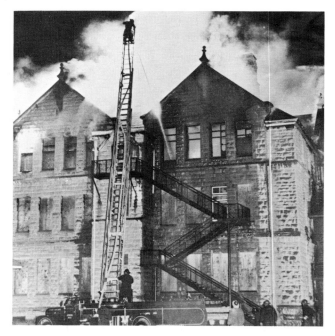

Haultain School, 13th Avenue and 2nd Street S.W., May 12, 1964.

Co-op Dairy Barn, 10th Avenue and 7th Street S.W., October 25, 1950.

Crystal Rink and Pool, 4th Avenue and 9th Street S.W., November 27, 1965.

Michael Building, 9th Avenue and 3rd Street S.W., January 21, 1966.

Davidman Furniture, 100 Block-1st Avenue S.E., March 14, 1949.

Great West Saddlery, 212-9th Avenue S.W., February 6, 1922.

Parisian, 106-8th Avenue S.E., October 7, 1973.

Beachcomber, 7th Avenue and 5th Street S.W., April 19, 1972.

Club Cafe, 100 Blk., 8 Ave. S.W. January 9, 1946.

White Lunch Roseroom, 221-225 8 Ave. S.W. January 10, 1962.

Maple Leaf Mills, 17 Ave. 14 St. S.E. April 19, 1968.

York Hotel, 7th Avenue and Centre Street S.W., November 20, 1970.

Commercial Bldg., 211-11th Ave. S.W., May 1, 1982.

General Hospital, 841 Centre Ave. East April 9, 1978.

Langevin School, 1 Ave. and 6A St. N.E. March 2, 1966.

Lone Pine Club, 19 Ave. and 53 St. S.W. August 13, 1965.

The Burns plant fire started at an early morning hour on Sunday, January 12, 1913, and burned for days, to qualify as Calgary's "worst fire" to that time and for many years to come. Writers called it Calgary's first million dollar fire although it was entered in the Fire Department records as a $900,000 disaster

Main Plant.

Storage Area.

Sides of Beef.

— which was probably close enough to a million dollars. Strangely enough both Chief Cappy Smart who was recuperating from injuries sustained in a street crash when going to a fire, and Pat Burns who was on a business trip in Eastern Canada, missed the awful conflagration. When Proprietor Pat Burns returned four days after the fire started — coming by train which was the only means available — the fire was still smoldering and the Waterous steam engine which had been in continuous action, 24 hours a day, was still pumping water on the ruins.

Waterous steam pumper.

Cappy having sand bath in Hawaii during Burns packing plant fire.

Clearly, the firemen had been working against terrible odds. It seemed to be impossible to maintain proper water pressure and, worse still, the bitterly cold January weather with temperatures ranging between zero and 30 below zero Fahrenheit, placed firemen in an almost impossible position. Water lines froze repeatedly, necessitating removal of the hose for thawing. When returned to service before they could be dried out, the hoses would freeze again. Firemen discovered what it was like to be unpleasantly hot in front and freezing behind. They experienced, also, the necessity of having to be practically "chopped out" of frozen clothing at the end of shifts.

Ice formation at Burns' fire.

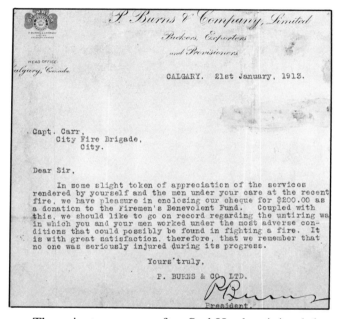

Then, just one year after Syd Hughes joined the Calgary Fire Brigade — where he was to serve for 38 years and rise to the rank of Battalion Chief — he was on front line action against the Sherman Rink fire. The big rink at the corner of 17th Avenue and Centre Street, gained a substantial start before the brigade was called and there was then no hope of doing more than recovering some of the contents and preventing the spread of the flames to nearby buildings.

Sherman Roller Rink, 17th Avenue and Centre Street S.W., January 25, 1915.

Fireman Hughes became engaged in carrying furniture and framed pictures from the rink quarters in which Lloyd Turner of hockey fame was living. Many of the pictures recovered when heat and smoke were growing in intensity, hung conspicuously in later years on the walls of the concourse of the Calgary Stampede Corral.

Everybody who had a part in battling the fire at the Empire hotel on 9th Avenue between Centre and 1st Street East, agreed that the stubborn nature of the blaze coupled with the intense cold and the high cost in both lives and dollars, made it most memorable. The temperature when the alarm was sounded at 3 a.m. was 28 below and wind and snow were threatening a blizzard. Syd Hughes was directed to search the burning building as far as he could go for occupants who might be trapped. He remembered the poker room with cards, chips and money left on the tables. He gathered the money, thinking somebody would claim it, but nobody did. Fire damage was placed at $137,346 and worst of all, three lives were lost.

Several of the C.F.D. veterans carried vivid memories of the $76,000 fire at the Wales hotel and annex in 1941. Nobody died but as Fireman William Hamilton recalled, at least one guest had a narrow and embarrassing escape. The alarm was received about 10:30 p.m., just after the bar was closed and Fireman Hamilton as operator of the Magirus aerial ladder truck with reach of 85 feet, arrived minutes later, by which time smoke was issuing from the main entrance of the hotel.

The hotel and annex were evacuated and not too soon because flames broke through a wall of the basement beauty parlor into an old elevator shaft and roared instantly up the shaft to involve all floors to the roof of the annex. The spread of the fire through the main part of the hotel was checked by water from the hose lines and Assistant Chief Jack McKinnon instructed Hamilton to set the aerial ladder on 7th Avenue to permit a "water tower" operation, meaning an attack from above.

But before the ladder was moved, the order was changed in haste to take a position on the street to rescue a man seen standing at a fourth floor window, shouting excitedly to have somebody move his car from the front of the hotel, as if more concerned about the car than himself. He wanted to throw his car keys to somebody who would move the car. But before the keys were thrown, the ladder was in place and two firemen climbed to assist the stranded man.

After moving the precious car, the stranger admitted that he had been asleep in his room, undisturbed by the fire alarm and general commotion until awakened by smoke. Only then did he realize his dilemma and was thinking excitedly about, first, having his car moved and, second, making a jump.

Mr. Hamilton said: "The most memorable part of the fire was the rapid spread of the flames through the building due to the old covered elevator shaft that acted like a chimney, spreading the fire to each floor on its way to the roof."

The burning of the Cameron block at the corner of 8th Avenue and 1st Street East, where Bob Edwards of the Calgary Eye Opener lived and wrote copy for many years, was memorable because it was unyielding and claimed seven lives.

Cameron Block, 8th Avenue and 1st Street S.E., November 29, 1961.

But every fire is different and the one that destroyed the No. 5 hangar, 30 planes and one glider at the Municipal Airport — a $2,500,000 loss — certainly wasn't to be forgotten. The fire broke at 9 p.m. and the flames that shot upward for 200 feet and continued through most of the night were seen for many miles, making this one of the most spectacular as well as costly. The hangar was owned by the Government of Canada and leased to the Calgary Flying Club that owned most of the planes. Said Manager William Smith, sadly, "It took us 25 years to build up the club and it took the fire only 25 minutes to break it down."[1]

The Calgary firemen who were around at the time, would never forget the Union Packing Company fire that resulted in the death of the highly respected Captain Arthur Simmons and sent four firemen to hospital. A cloud of sorrow fell upon the city.

Making the situation additionally treacherous, an explosion soon after the fire started on the Wednesday evening released volumes of ammonia and blanketed the area with dangerous fumes. Eighteen hours after the $213,000 blaze started, firemen were still on the job, still wearing smoke masks.

It was Captain Simmons' misfortune while leading the attack against the fire to fall, unnoticed by his men, through the hatch of a cellar used for storing hides. With visibility diminished by smoke, the other firemen were not immediately aware that the Captain was not with them. As soon as they realized what had happened, they pulled him from the cellar and administered first aid. But the popular fellow, suffering from fumes and perhaps concussion, failed to regain consciousness and died at the General Hospital several hours later.

The Calgary Herald editorialized fittingly, pointing up some timely truths: "The death of Captain Arthur Simmons of the Calgary Fire Department, killed in performance of his duty, is a forceful reminder that death and injury are never far from a firefighter's side. The gallant man, a veteran of the First Great War, followed the best traditions of his force."

"Captain Simmons is the second city fireman to give his life in service. Fireman Hugh McShane was fatally injured on October 29, 1923, when a fire truck crashed into an electric light pole when returning home from a prairie fire. Many members of the department have been injured while fighting fires and some of them will bear the scars to their graves."

"It can be said that a firefighter takes a calculated risk. He is trained not only in fighting fire, but in the avoidance of unnecessary danger. But all risks cannot be calculated. The firefighter may be overcome by fumes. He may be crushed by a suddenly falling wall or by beams. And he may, like Fireman McShane, be killed going to or coming from a fire. The irony of the situation is that the biggest fire is not necessarily the most dangerous."[2]

No. 5 Hangar, Airport, December 6, 1954.

Calgary Firefighters Who Died In Service

Firefighter H. McShane — **1919-1923**
Joined C.F.D. — April 25, 1919
Died — Nov. 17, 1923 — Traffic Accident with Apparatus

Captain A. Simmons — **1911-1948**
Joined C.F.D. — Jan. 31, 1911
Died — Dec. 30, 1948 — Union Packing Plant Fire

Firefighter N. Cocks — **1957-1962**
Joined C.F.D. — Dec. 16, 1957
Died — May 8, 1962 — Drill at #1 Station

Lieutenant L. Dutnall — **1952-1970**
Joined C.F.D. — Feb. 25, 1952
Died — Sept. 6, 1970 — Calgary Stockyards Fire

Lieutenant H. Smith — **1952-1971**
Joined C.F.D. — June 2, 1952
Died — May 27, 1971 — McTavish Block Fire
Lieutenant Smith was also a Firefighter from May 7, 1945 to Jan. 16, 1952.

Firefighter J. Walters — **1971-1972**
Joined C.F.D. — Feb. 15, 1971
Died — Apr. 19, 1972 — Beachcomber Night Club Fire

Firefighter D. Allan — **1960-1976**
Joined C.F.D. — June 13, 1960
Died — Aug. 25, 1976 — Traffic Accident with Apparatus

Firefighter G. Look — **1979-1981**
Joined C.F.D. — Sept. 4, 1979
Died — Jan. 1, 1981 — Manchester Racquet Club Fire

Some of the most memorable fires were beyond the city limits, it being the view of Cappy Smart and others that municipal boundaries should not stand in the way when neighbors need help. In the annual report for 1930, the C.F.D. listed 14 out-of-city points as far as Rockyford, Black Diamond, Crossfield, and Ghost River to which help was sent.[3]

The earliest country expedition was a hurried one to High River in January, 1906. A special train carried the steam pumper, hose and 13 firemen including Cappy Smart. On the High River fire front an hour after getting the call, the engine forced Highwood River water on the flames for two hours and then the fire was out and the men turned to home.

A fire at Crossfield was memorable because the Calgary firemen saw the town three times in one night, the first time to deal with the fire in a livery stable and lumber yard, the second time when called back to extinguish a new blaze in an adjacent building, and the third time when, as Joe Fitts recalled, the half frozen men were informed at Airdrie, that the Chief's car was off the road and stuck in the snow at Crossfield.

None of the veterans consulted in 1983 had taken part in the High River adventure of 1906 but several, including Joe Fitts who as the motor mechanic, went where the motors went, had clear recollections of the fast and furious trip to Banff in 1921.[4] The message relayed through D. C. Coleman who was then Divi-

sional Superintendent for the C.P.R., requested help to combat the fire which was out of control at the elegant Banff Springs Hotel, owned by the C.P.R. The superintendent would supply a special train at once if the Calgary firemen would come with good apparatus.

Within minutes, it seemed, a pumper was loaded on a freight car and the men were invited to occupy the superintendent's private car, hooked behind the flat car. The chef had breakfast ready and the men dined as the train took off at a speed that was unprecedented. The cars rocked and swayed as if about to jump the track. Fitts said "we got more egg on our laps than in our stomachs." But the fire engine and men were at the scene of the fire in an hour and 40 minutes after leaving Calgary and remained for six hours when the job was completed. Said Joe Fitts: "I answered quite a few calls to neighboring towns but never did I make such a wild trip as the one to Banff."

[1] Calgary Herald, Dec. 7, 1954.
[2] Calgary Herald, Dec. 31, 1948.
[3] Calgary Fire Department, 1930.
[4] Fitts, Joe, Recollections of C.F.D. under eight chiefs, 1916 to 1958, 1974.

Banff Springs Hotel, Banff, Alberta, 1921 (Rear View).

Banff Springs Hotel.

Didsbury business district, Didsbury, Alberta, January 2, 1914.

Didsbury Main Street.

Cold Weather Firefighting

"I dread these cold snaps".

Alarm
of
Fire

Townhouses, 11th Avenue and 15th Street S.W., August 21, 1982.

Deerfoot Shopping Mall, 901-64th Avenue N.E., March 28, 1981.

Deerfoot Shopping Mall, 901-64th Avenue N.E., March 28, 1981.

IKO fire, 1603-42nd Avenue S.E., October 8, 1980.

IKO fire, 1603-42nd Avenue S.E., October 8, 1980.

IKO fire, 1603-42nd Avenue S.E., October 8, 1980.

Windsor Park School, 5505-4A Street S.W., February 11, 1975.

Windsor Park School, 5505-4A Street S.W., February 11, 1975.

House fire.

Burritt Travel, 327-8 Ave. S.W.

Action Muffler, 4121 Macleod Trail South, November 30, 1976.

Premier Laundry, 905-3rd Avenue S.W., April 27, 1978.

Michael Building, 9 Ave. 3 St. S.W. January 21, 1966.

House explosion.

Cameron Block, 8th Avenue and 1st Street S.E., November 29, 1961.

Town Houses, 11th Avenue and 15th Street S.W., August 21, 1982.

House under construction, 35th Ave. and 29 St. S.W.

Airport Hangar fire, May 14, 1983.

Hangar and Aircraft fire, Airport, May 14, 1983.

95

Old Martin's Bakery, 605-35th Avenue N.E., March 20 1981.

Old Martin's Bakery fire; pumper scorched due to intense heat.

Firebird in operation.

Motor vehicle roll over accident.

Commercial Building, 211-11th Avenue S.W., May 1, 1982.

Warehouse 5719-6 St. S.E. December 28, 1983.

Firebird in operation.

Firefighters fight fire in abandoned house that may have been used by transients.

Glengarry School, 2019-29th Street S.W., September 20, 1978.

200 Block, 8th Avenue S.E., January 17, 1984.

Apartment Fire, 10th Street N.W., June 13, 1984.

Tanker fire on Deerfoot Trail, May 6, 1984.

Sungold Manufacturing, 550 Southland Drive S.W., November 23, 1977.

Sungold Manufacturing.

Sungold Manufacturing.

Sun Gold Manufacturing.

Sun Gold Manufacturing.

Residential fire.

Residential fire.

Travel Trailer.

Clark Roofing, 3915-2nd Street N.E., March 11, 1981.

Old Calgary Herald building, August 9, 1984.

Abandoned house.

Farmer's Market, 3810 Blackfoot Trail S.E., June 13, 1983.

Large grass fire west of Strathcona Heights, Spring, 1984.

The Self-Help Wonder Grew

Resourcefulness is a fireman's badge and he wears it proudly. It was the spirit of ingenuity that led the Fire Chief of 1913, while addressing a request to the Mayor for more motorized equipment to say, in effect: "If the budget will not permit the purchase of the fire trucks which we need, please buy some one-ton chassis — new or second hand — and our own mechanics working in our own shop will build the bodies."

Early equipment (hose wagon) converted in C.F.D. shop.

The desired pieces of running gear with motors were obtained ultimately and the men in the machine shop did the rest, thereby furnishing the city with a fleet of specialized firefighting apparatus at an average saving to the city of $2,000 per unit. Commenting on these homemade fire trucks, Motor Mechanic Joe Fitts said: "At one time we had a Fiat, a Rocket-Schneider, a Kissel, a Winton, a Model T Ford and

1909 Rochet Schneider purchased by C.F.D. in 1912 converted to a hose wagon.

an early Buick," all of which had been touring cars before they were firefighting vehicles.[1]

So it was in 1902 when members of the Volunteer Fire Department recognized a need for some form of financial security for themselves and those who followed whose lives were frought with uncommon risks and dangers. The outcome was the organization of the Calgary Firemens' Benefit Association, a self-help effort that would guarantee financial aid in the event of serious injuries and specified contributions toward funeral expenses in case of death.

Firemen came to the service with varied backgrounds of race, education and occupations and some did not stay long. But those who remained were quickly drawn together and held by bonds of resourcefulness, loyalty and co-operation, a point demonstrated most clearly in the organization and mounting success of the Calgary Fire Fighters' Credit Union in 1941. The country was just recovering from the paralyzing effects of the great depression that gained added intensity by the succession of drought years in the West.

Firemen receiving modest wages and trying to buy homes and achieve a measure of independence were experiencing money management problems. The recognized lending institutions, still reeling from the financial troubles of the '30s, were being administered with extreme caution and firemen began talking about Credit Unions which had been tried elsewhere with apparent success in meeting the needs of working people. A few Calgary firemen reasoned that such a self-help enterprise should do especially well in a relatively compact occupational group like the city firemen. Said W. D. Craig who watched the Credit Union develop and was helpful to it: "It seemed that the conditions under which the firefighters were working, ideally met the important criteria of close working bonds and common needs. All members could benefit through participation in a financial business of this nature operated by themselves and for themselves."[2]

A small group of firemen, recognizing that the social and economic climate of the time was favorable for a co-operative venture, decided to act. It was a lowly beginning, a point finding proof in the testimony of Former Chief W. D. Craig, that the incorporation fee for the proposed organization was collected from 10 of the enthusiastic ones who donated 25 cents each. The founding 10 or charter members were listed as: C. Eastwood, A. Lucas, W. G. Taylor, G. Swales, S. Prynn, W. Hamilton, W. Martin, C. Giroux, J. Robertson, and E. Brotherton.

The infant Credit Union, operating out of No. 1 Fire Hall, was ready for business at the end of 1941. The first Individual Share and Loan Ledger shows Fireman G. R. Austin, 423 15th St. N.W. as starting to make share payments on January 15. The first two payments in January were of 50 cents each. In February, the original client paid $4.00 and by April 6, 1943, he had share equity of $17.50. But on March 2, 1942, he obtained a loan of $50.00 undertaking to repay at the rate of $2.50 each half month starting March 31st. The payments were made faithfully twice a month until September 15 when the debt was fully paid and the borrower's cost in interest compiled every two weeks totalled $2.95. The amounts of the customer's transactions by later standards will seem humorously small but they were no doubt useful to Mr. Austin and he would be grateful to the Credit Union.

Most deposits and loans for the first year were small but important to somebody. The Credit Union's total assets at the end of the first year were $1,189,

certainly not very impressive but from that time forward, deposits and loans escalated at a spectacular rate and by 1960 when the operation was moved to its own building at 114, 5th Avenue, S.E., the Credit Union had become a $400,000 annual business. The next move to bigger quarters at 227 12th Avenue, S.E. was in 1971. And again, with growing business and expanding needs, a still bigger and more pretentious building was constructed on an adjoining 12th Avenue site. The latter, a $1,705,000 structure officially opened on June 5, 1981, was built with foundations to carry additional floors which, it was supposed, would be needed before many years.

Credit Union members with a good sense of thrift were pleased to be informed when the plans for the new office headquarters were presented in 1980, that "it [the building] will be completely paid for by 1984."[3]

When the 30th anniversary was being marked in 1971, the Calgary Firefighters' Credit Union was granting 2,080 loans for a total of $1,189,364 and showing a share capital of more than a million dollars. Such totals would not be impressively large on the books of a national bank doing business with large firms and industries but when they are seen as the dealings of working people who desire "to save together and lend to each other at reasonable rates," they mean service as well as business.

In showing the reasons why clients sought loans in that 30th year of the Credit Union, the management was inadvertently explaining in a most enlightening manner a basic role and a basic reason for

Calgary Firefighters Credit Union, 215-12th Avenue S.E.

the operation of a Credit Union. The loans obtained in 1971 were for the following declared purposes:[4]

Purpose For Loan	Number of Loans	Cash Loaned
Consolidation of debts	795	$260,354.75
Auto repair and purchase	510	281,870.53
School	48	26,098.00
Medical, dental	21	6,165.00
Vacation	286	45,863.00
Building improvement	213	415,777.84
Land	18	27,500.00
Household equipment	27	14,740.00
Taxes	47	15,768.48
Christmas	38	12,407.00
Miscellaneous	77	82,819.45
Total	2,080	$1,189,364.05

And still the firemens' do-it-yourself wonder grew. As seen on the occasion of the annual meeting in 1982, President Les Badry could point out for directors and members that their Credit Union which finished its first year exactly 40 years earlier with total assets of less than $1,200, completed the recent year with deposits of $15,736,721 and total assets of $19,618,361.[5]

As the annual report was being presented, it was not being overlooked that the Canadian economy was experiencing a major recession and the Credit Union was, in consequence, "sailing in choppy waters" and adjusting to "the higher risk potential." But the Credit Union's security was still high enough to be the envy of most other financial institutions. Existing for service more than profit and having roughly 90 per cent of the Calgary firemen as members, with not many of the country's big speculative borrowers who can be most vulnerable in times of recession and depression, the Credit Union's position remained relatively safe and sound.

In the general area of group organization, the Calgary Firefighters' Credit Union, Ltd., affiliated with the Credit Union League of Alberta and the Credit Union National Association, was still appearing as one of the worthy showpieces.

Long before Credit Unions were commonplace, Calgary firemen organized one of the more familiar self-help labor unions, hoping it would strengthen their bargaining position with their employers. Working conditions in the years after 1909 when the volunteer firemen were replaced by full time and fully paid workers, left much to be desired. Joe Fitts who entered the service in 1916, wrote: "I became No. 75 and was on duty 24 hours a day for six days a week with one hour off for each meal. . . . My salary was $69.37 per month, less $5.00 for the Red Cross."[6]

It wasn't surprising that firemen on duty for 126 hours per week hoped the influence of a Union would bring some relief. The first Union president, A. E. Crocket, and secretary, J. Shearer, wrote to the Fire Chief on February 19, 1917, to advise him that the organization of the Calgary Fire Fighters' Federal Union had been completed and asked permission for the use of a basement room in a fire hall to be Union headquarters until permanent quarters could be obtained. He explained the new Union's affiliation with the Canadian Trades Congress, the Calgary local of which was headed at the time by the highly regarded Elmer E. Roper, later Member of the Legislature and Mayor of Edmonton.

The idea of a Firemens' Union received a mixed reception by the public and brought some editorial protests. But the protesters had nothing to fear and the Calgary firemen, working shorter hours, continued to enjoy the public confidence. One year after that initial Firefighters' Union was formed at Calgary, the International Association of Firefighters was formed at Washington, D.C., and the Calgary body, henceforward to be known as the Calgary Firefighters' Union, No. 255, became affiliated on October 4, 1923.

As shown by the Constitution and By-Laws of both the International Association and local Union, it would have been difficult for fair-minded people to disagree with the independence and high purposes sounded by the respective organizations. Sections one and two of the Calgary Union are presented herewith as deserving of study by members of the public: "The object of this Union shall be the fostering and encouragement of a higher degree of skill and efficiency, the cultivation of friendship and fellowship among its members, the maintenance of proper remuneration for duty performed, and the elevation and improvement of the moral, intellectual, social and economic conditions of its members."

"It shall be deemed inadvisable to strike, or take active part in strikes, as our position is peculiar to most organized workers, as we are formed to protect the lives and property of the community in case of fire or other serious hazards."[7]

It is noteworthy that Calgary in 67 years after the local Union was organized, never had a firemens' strike although only in the latter part of the period was the city covered by provincial legislation outlawing strikes in the highly essential occupations.

Robert G. Williams who was president of Local 255 for 11 years — 1966 to 1977 — speaking with pride in the Union's record, said: "Consultation is better than confrontation. We have always tried to make arbitration work."

Local 255, I.A.F.F., Calgary Firefighters Association, 538-7th Avenue S.E.

A city official, after reporting the firemens' decision when the city, early in 1983 was facing a financial crisis, to accept a delay in promised wage increases in order to save the jobs of 35 junior firemen from layoff, said: "The members of Local 255 have always shown mature judgment; it makes them nice to deal with."[8]

The Credit Union and the Firefighters' Union had self-help motives, quite obviously, which is legitimate enough. But there were other organizations bespeaking their members' versatility and charity. One of these with the most unselfish of purposes, the Firefighters' Burn Treatment Society, must be mentioned.

Firemen in the regular course of their duties, will see the savage cruelty of fire, often causing intense suffering, sometimes death, sometimes disfigurement for life. Many times sympathetic firemen asked: "Can more be done to ease the suffering and heal the wounds?" "What could we do to hasten recovery?" Hearing of occasions when extra money would buy new medical aids or treatment, they decided to establish a fund to be used exclusively for the relief and cure of burns.

The Firefighters' Burn Treatment Society was organized and the application for incorporation was signed by the Society President, Walter Kruschel and seven other officers and directors in November, 1978, and the certificate of incorporation was delivered later in the same month.

The Burn Society has been conducted without fanfare and without public appeals but members — all from the Calgary Fire Department — obtain contributions and gifts and make contributions and gifts sufficient to pay for a service that brings much quiet satisfaction to those who have guided it and have strong feeling for it.

H. Moore presenting cheque on behalf of firefighters to Muscular Dystrophy president, Jesse Church.

B. Pedersen presenting cheque to Foothills Hospital burn treatment unit on behalf of the Firefighters Toy Association.

[1] Fitts, Joe, Recollections, unpublished, dated Nov. 18, 1974.
[2] Craig, W. D., Historical sketch of Calgary Firefighters' Credit Union, Unpublished, 1983.
[3] Report, Annual Meeting of Calgary Firefighters' Credit Union, Feb. 4, 1980.
[4] Report, Annual Meeting of Calgary Firefighters' Credit Union, 1972.
[5] Annual Report, Calgary Firefighters' Credit Union, for 1982, Feb. 1983.
[6] Fitts, Joe, Recollections, unpublished, written Nov., 1974.
[7] Calgary Firefighters' Union, No. 255, By-Laws, Calgary, 1938.
[8] Calgary Herald, Jan. 13, 1983.

Pioneers In Public Relations

Community involvement extending far beyond fire related duties was, for men of the Calgary Fire Department, like a golden thread that remained unbroken for a hundred years. As pioneers with good memories told many times, the brigade from its inception was "at the centre of things in Calgary." Even the volunteer members with little more than buckets, axes and good intentions with which to work, were marked and influential men. An early candidate for the office of mayor admitted that his biggest handicap was in the fact that the men of the Fire Brigade refused to support him.

No doubt that good relationship between citizens and the firemen was easier to achieve when the city was small and it was inevitable that people would know each other better. In any case, the bonds of fellowship were strong and the Fire Hall was a place at which men and women and boys and girls felt at home.

Every town or city needed a hub or centre with doors open to all. In homestead districts, the livery stables and pool rooms were the only "drop-in" centres but they were for men only and the out-of-town ladies were left commonly with no place at which to turn in for a few minutes of relaxation. In Calgary, both men and women were quick to take advantage of their fire hall with an imposing bell tower and an open door on McIntyre Avenue, a convenient place at which to meet a friend or leave a message or take refuge from winter cold or borrow a ladder.

Oh those ladders! The brigade's ladders were the best ones in town and became so popular with borrowers that when the volunteer firemen responded to a fire alarm one day in 1892, not a single ladder remained where it belonged and a stern order had to be issued: "No more ladders to be removed except for reasons of fire."

Back Row, L-R: Brooks, Unknown, Ashcroft, Smart, Mayor Adams, McDougall, Booth, Poulton. Front Row: Burns, Newstead, Barker, Launders, Carr, Dawson, Richardson, Murray, Gaylord.

Harry B. Wilson who joined as a volunteer fireman in 1889, said the fire hall became the town's social centre. There the firemen organized picnics, concerts and athletic events. They would meet any challenge to field a team for soccer, baseball, lacrosse, hockey or tug of war. Soccer and baseball were the most popular at that time and the Calgary Fire Department won coveted trophies in both.

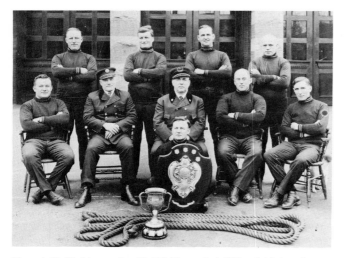

Rear, L-R: E. Alexander, C. Whitbread, J. Fitts, J. Livingstone. Front: Unknown, A. Carr, Cappy Smart, J. Shelley, G. Skene. Behind shield: G. Rosam.

Back, L-R: G. Rivers, E. Prince, M. Walker, R. Dolan, G. Dancer. Front: D. Martin, D. Coates, R. Renard, G. Young.

Calgary Fire Brigade Association Football Team, Winners of Cochrane Trophy 1896 and Doll Trophy 1895. Back, L-R: G. Mitchell, Ex-Chief J. Wilson, D. Lloyd, Chief H. McClelland, J. Tom, T. Bruce. Middle: C. Comer, A. Boyd, J. Smart, G. Baetz, G. Henderson. Front: R. Chipman. T. Tarrant.

C.F.D. Hockey Champions, 1894-95. Back, L-R: E. Marshall, S. Saunders, J. Wilson (chief), R. Chipman, C. Comer. Front: H. Watson, T. Bruce, F. Atkins, G. Henderson.

Industrial Hockey League Champions. Kyle Bros. Trophy was presented to Division Chief Percy Simmons. Back Row, L-R: F. Popovich, R. Parr, R. Kilroe, P. MacMillan, N. Cave, P. Simmons, C. Yahn, V. Bannon, S. Steer, J. Johnson. Front Row: R. English, R. Brooks, B. Milton, W. Beattie, S. Brooks, W. McAndrews, J. Bradshaw.

FIRE   DEPT.

Rock Crawford
Left Wing

George Kubicek
Right Wing

Roy Brooks
Goal

Geo Gerlitz
Defence

Roy Rust
Right Wing

Mick Gilday
Centre

Bill Phillips
Trainer

Tommy Head
Coach

Cliff Davis
Manager

Gerry Minton
Defence

Don Clark
Centre

Frank Golembrosky
Stick boy

Jim Keats
Centre

Jim Anderson
Right Wing

Bill Malcolm
Left Wing

Bruno Ruchryn
Left Wing

Ted Stewart
Defence

Bob Moore
Defence

'61–'62   CHAMPIONS

— LLOYD TURNER TROPHY —

Senger Photo

Back Row, L-R: J. McDougall, H. Dawson, C. Eastwood, D. Clenchy, D. Finlayson, N. Strang, A. Stuggart, T. Greengrove, G. Fox, G. Murray. Middle Row: R. Ferguson, T. Head, G. Wasilinchuk, C. Hicklin, B. Cyr, F. Dougan, G. Alexander. Front Row: S. Steer, Hicklin J. Carrington.

Dominion Firefighters Curling Champions, Winnipeg, 1975. C. Braren, D. Nelson, J. MacMillan, T. Wych.

Plowing match: Harry Tucker, Bill McLaughlin.

CALGARY FIRE DEPT.
City Intermediate Hockey League Champions
1946-1947
Winning All League and Exhibition Games Played During Season

Calgary Fire Department versus Edmonton Fire Department annual baseball game.

Provincial Hose Laying Competition, First Place: Ron Spielman, Stu Wurster, Fred Robinson, Rock Kilroe.

1949 Baseball Champions. Front Row, L-R: C. Hicklin, Chief J. Shelley, Deputy Chief P. Brooks, A. McCallum. Middle Row: D. Craig, C. Davey, R. Cyr, J. Cook, T. Davidson, S. Steer. Back Row: J. McDougall, C. Biggs, D. Finaylson, N. Strang, L. Brown, D. Clenchy, J. Carrington.

1952 Hose Laying Champions. Back Row: J. Weatherly, J. Waters. Front Row: A. Flaig, G. Lang.

D. Craig opening curling season.

Baseball Team, 1948. Back Row, L-R: H. Glover, J. Cook, S. Brooks, C. Davey, S. Steer, R. Cundy, L. Brown, D. Finlayson. Front Row: D. Craig, M. Cummins, J. McDougall, B. Silver. Mascot: Frankie Chow.

Northwest Police and Firefighters Olympics, Gold Medal Winners, Edmonton, 1983. Top Row, L-R: K. Wanvig, B. Daniel, T. Wych, G. Williams, G. Simpson, J. Ingram, D. Rabel, W. McQueen, P. Halas, G. Young. Front Row: G. Pozzo, M. Crawford, D. Huber, R. Stevenson, F. Deiure, J. Keats. Missing: B. Duncan, T. Newcombe, D. Freeman. Bat Boys: K. Ingram (missing), M. Pozzo, K. Wanvig.

Calgary Firefighters Old Timers Hockey

Calgary Fire Department Old Timers, 1978-1979. Back Row, L-R: B. Milton (cach), P. Kaiser, D. Wagner, G. Brown, G. Young, G. Minton, S. Hendry, B. Willis, R. Crawford. Middle Row: G. Caron, D. Huggard, B. Weslosky, J. Keats, D. Blomquist, P. Halas, J. Walker, G. Evans, B. Kuchtyn. Front Row: L. Thompson, T. Stewart, J. MacLellan, G. Kubicek, R. Spycher, D. Silvernagle, T. Cochlan, T. Faulkner, M. Gilday, T. Bell. Missing: B. Beattie, B. Duncan, A. Gummo, B. Zoback, M. McGurk.

Calgary Firefighters Old Timers, 1979-1980. Back Row, L-R: G. Simpson, G. Evans, H. Stewart, A. Gummo, G. Caron, T. Bell, L. Thompson. Middle Row: T. Faulkner, J. Walker, D. Huggard, D. Blomquist, B. Bjornson, B. Zoback, P. Halas, J. MacLellan. Front Row: G. Young, J. Keats, B. Duncan, T. Stewart, W. Morris, B. Milton (coach), G. Brown (manager).

For some years, the annual Firemens' Ball, held at the New Year's season or on St. Patrick's Day was the unquestioned highlight of the social season. And for a longer period of years, the 24th of May sports program organized by the Calgary firemen was the biggest thing of its kind west of Winnipeg. Of the ball held on December 30, 1890, the press reported that dancing began at 9 p.m. and continued until 3 a.m., with an intermission for supper at midnight. One hundred and twenty guests attended and the music was the best that Calgarians had ever heard.[1]

Hull's Opera House.

By this time, the Calgary Fire Department had its own band, formed earlier in the year and bandsmen were now making their first public appearance in recently acquired uniforms. The men, it seems, began negotiating for uniforms but before a purchase had been made, a generous Calgary business man and rancher, D. W. Marsh, came forward and presented a full supply of uniforms he bought from the Oddfellows Lodge, along with some instruments.

In the next year, 1891, the Fire Brigade, proud of its band and still eager to be diversifying its services to the community, undertook to build a bandstand in the C.P.R. park, east of the locations at which the depot and Palliser hotel were to stand later.

The reputation of the Brigade band in which both firemen and non-firemen played together, travelled far. In 1902, playing under the leadership of Crispen Smith, it was judged the best in the Northwest and it was invited to present a concert at the bandstand on September 1, 1905, to mark the birth of the Province on that date.[2]

The annual sports program presented on the 24th of May came very much under the direction of Chief Cappy Smart and was considered the biggest and best in the West. The event of 1905 was typical. Special trains brought 800 visitors from as far north as Edmonton and as far south as Fort Macleod. Naturally, there was a wild scramble to find sufficient hotel or substitute accommodation.

Firemen's Ball, Hull's Opera House.

Trophies and Awards of the Calgary Fire Department

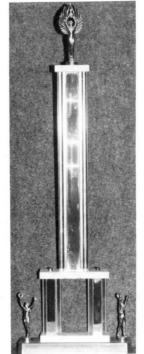

Nine bands were present and all or nearly all took part in the opening parade that started, as always, close to the Fire Hall on McIntyre Avenue. The parade moved away when Chief Smart fired his starting pistol and it ended at Victoria Park where most of the day's competitions were conducted. City Fire Brigade vehicles took part and members of visiting athletic teams marched to make it the biggest parade seen on Calgary streets to that time. Exploding firecrackers made parade horses want to run away and spectators were treated to a few unscheduled bucking performances. Fakirs could not resist the chance of setting up along the route for some fortune telling and the sale of sure-cure medicines. It was a sports day with a carnival atmosphere.

1935 Stampede Parade.

1899 · The C.F.B. Band
In 1901, the first Fire Department Church Parade was held and the first bandstand was erected in the City by the Fire Department at the old C.P.R. Port on Atlantic Avenue.

1899 C.F.D. Band.

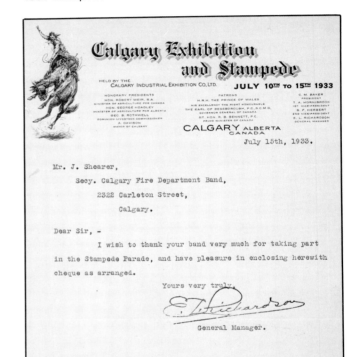

1909 Fire Chief's Convention.

Calgary Fire Department Mewata Days Demonstration

"SUGAR PLUM FAIRIES"

Sugar Plum Fairies. Back, L-R: E. McKay, J. Brosh, G. Huskinson. Front: G. Young, C. Lefurgey.

Calgary's Finest — In 1901. Back: (third from left) the late Dr. George MacDonald, (eighth from left) "Scotty" Lloyd, (ninth from left) "Ed" Hall, (tenth from left) Capt. H. B. Wilson, (eleventh from left) "Billy" Smith, (twelfth from left) the late E. J. Young. Front: (second from left) S. L. Saunders, (third) Alf May, (fourth) former Fire Chief "Cappy" Smart, (fifth) Crispin E. Smith, bandmaster, (sixth) "Ed" McConkie, drum major, (eighth) Charlie Whitehead. Seated: (left) Harry Murphy, trap drummer, (right) George Henderson.

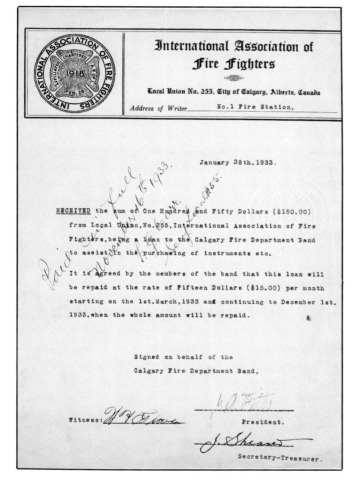

In the evening, the Fire Brigade competitions were staged on McIntyre Avenue, in front of the Fire Hall. Hose reel races were the feature events and the Calgary team, being the custodian of the trophy cup after having won it in the previous year, did not enter the initial contest but after watching the Strathcona firemen win the race, the Calgary men challenged the current winners and won the right to keep the trophy. But the Calgary Brigade's tug of war team did not do quite so well and had to be satisfied with second prize.

An innovation near the end of the program consisted of a presentation of a gold locket "From the City of Calgary to John Smart for heroic services, 1905." This Smart was one of three of Cappy Smart's brothers who served with the Brigade and the heroic service was in the capture of a runaway team of green fire horses.[3]

One way or another, community involvement beyond the call of duty was encouraged by Chief Smart and the Chiefs who followed and it became established as a brigade tradition. Brigade teams in baseball, soccer and hockey continued to be prominent in local leagues for many years and when midget teams needed a coach or referee, they could always find one at the fire hall.

Only those who lived close to fire stations knew the firemens' willingness to help with junior athletics whether it was in flooding a rink or finding hockey sticks for youngsters who were unable to buy new ones.

In those years of depression when many parents could not afford even a barber's fees for cutting boys' hair, they discovered some firemen who were moderately handy with scissors and clippers. Any boy who visited one of several fire halls and asked politely, could get a free haircut. One of the boys, after growing to manhood, told that his first haircut at the fire hall was "pretty rough and left him looking as though the barber job was done with a jackknife." But the young customers were not fussy and kindly "barbers" improved until they were able to do a near professional job.

Towns and communities between Edmonton and Fort Macleod fought it out for tournament honors in baseball, soccer and tug of war and individuals from more distant points contested in races and other field events. Members of the Calgary Fire Department could enter as individuals and did. Neil McLaughlin who drove horse teams on the ladder wagons, including the three-horse team on the heavier wagon of later years, proved that he was the best man in that rugged Scottish sport, the tossing of the caber, "the trunk of a pine tree somewhat smaller than a telephone pole." McLaughlin's toss was measured at 24 feet, 9 inches and Calgarians — especially Scottish Calgarians — cheered with delight.

125

Fire fighting was a serious matter. Nobody disagreed. But there are times when everybody needs the relaxing effect of good laughs and no group did more in contributing to entertainment and laughter than the Calgary firemen. Clowning became an off-duty specialty and clown team popularity brought requests for appearances from many parts.

In 1972 the 10-man clown team was again travelling to Eastern Canada to take part in the annual Grey Cup parade in Hamilton, travelling this time under the sponsorship of Atco Industries. The actors, of course, were taking along their famous clown-created fire truck that was sure to catch almost as much attention as a Calgary quarterback.

Fireman Ian McLean who acted as the clown team's leader that year, explained how he and his men would spend a minimum of time in Ontario because their first resonsibility was to the Calgary Fire Department and, in addition, the team had a heavy booking of pre-Christmas engagements at schools, community centres, childrens' wards in hospitals and Christmas concerts and these were, in the firemens' view, more important than extended appearances at the football game.

By this time in 1972, the clown team was already almost 25 years old. For that length of time, the members had been generating healthy laughter and receiving close to 200 calls per year — and accepting most of them.

Charitable organizations turned many times to the men of the C.F.D. — still do — and nearly always found willing help. "The firemen will always listen," a churchman said.

Fund Raising Laughter at Mewata with the Calgary Fire Department

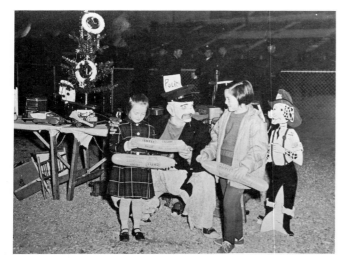

Department Clown and Friends.

Xmas hampers provided by Calgary Firefighters. Lieut. B. Pedersen presenting $5000.00 hamper fund to Salvation Army Capt. Merritt.

Night Hitch Race.

Save The Policeman.

Clowning in the snow.

Tijuana Toots, G. Young, B. Freney, D. Parish.

From participation as a clown team willing to help in worthy public causes, it was but a short step to entry in the comedy section of Edmonton's Sourdough Raft Races, held annually in conjunction with Klondike Days. Four Calgary firemen would accompany the raft invention to Edmonton and make the down-river voyage on the North Saskatchewan with this strange fire boat. Painted a bright yellow, the pumper fire engine puzzled people who were not aware of the official change of color from fire engine red to fire engine yellow or lemon back home in Calgary. But except for color, the aquatic fire apparatus depending for its buoyancy upon eight 45-gallon oil barrels, didn't look like anything in the very modern fleet of fire fighting machines back in Calgary.

It was a fine display of the ridiculous and the thousands of spectators lining the river bank for the distance of the raft races, were fascinated by the screaming of the fire engine siren in midstream, the flashing of the red danger lights and the great stream of water being forced high overhead, as if offering fire boat protection for the scores of very wet rafts if threatened by burning.

The Sunday afternoon viewers laughed and spoke appreciatively of the Calgary Fire Department, which was exactly what it was hoped they would do.

L-R: J. Swain, A. Lyons, W. McCaw, J. Thomas.

Merry Xmas at No. 27 Station.

Xmas at No. 10 Station.

It was another exercise in public relations, strongly suggestive of the way that firemen had been living in Calgary and community for more than three-quarters of a century as they responded to fire calls beyond the city, gave leadership in Christmas lighting, supported games and furnished the city's best Santa Claus program. And then, as if to confirm the importance of it all, Calgary's Fire Chief, Derek Jackson, announced the appointment of an official Public Affairs representative in the person of Captain Tom Davidson — a 27-year veteran of the force — to be officially responsible for ensuring understanding and good relations between the brigade on one hand and the press, radio, television and general public on the other.

Of course it was important to be on good terms with the community, as the C.F.D. had tried to be for many years — with success.

[1] Calgary Herald, Dec. 31, 1890.
[2] Calgary Herald, May 25, 1905.
[3] Calgary Herald, May 25, 1905.

Honour Guard. Front Row, L-R: J. Matlock, R. Choppe, F. Silliker, P. Robinson, M. Soehner, D. McPherson, B. Freney. Back Row: W. Mitchell, J. Baudistel, V. Sager, D. Fofonoff, K. Haines, L. Thompson, B. Gray.

Sparky, the C.F.D. mascot.

C.F.D. officially leaving old No. 1 Station at 6th Avenue and 1st Street S.E., turning it over to the Calgary Tourist and Convention Association.

C.F.D. bed race team.

Fire Department clowns: Sitting: Grant McQuarrie. Standing, L-R: Gary Haden, Tom Devey, Ian McLean.

Sparky at Alberta Children's Hospital.

Calgary Firefighters Of Distinction

Every occupation has its exceptional individuals about whom citizens who come later will talk and boast. Some like Gordie Howe of professional hockey, John W. Dafoe of journalism, Paddy Nolan of law and James "Cappy" Smart of firefighting became legends.

The Calgary Fire Department had a big share of the personalities that deserved to be enshrined in human memory. It would be a mistake to forget or ignore them and likewise, a mistake to attempt to treat all on these limited pages. Should an author draw names from a hat or simply attempt to select a few worthy and representative specimens and run the risk of criticism because some good candidates were omitted? The latter course is preferable but its pursuit must be with the full realization that there were other candidates who, for all practical purposes, were equally worthy of recognition.

The author did indeed seek advice and tried to follow it but he alone must bear the responsibility for the names now appearing on this short list of distinctive Calgary firefighters.

The James "Cappy" Smart story has been told many times and distorted a few times. But as a rare and entertaining personality as well as a progressive and successful fireman, he had one of the best claims to a place of prominence on any list of Calgarians or Canadians of Distinction.

But this man who arrived in Calgary in 1883 — the year of the railroad to that place — and began a half-century career in firefighting soon after arrival by joining the Hook, Ladder and Bucket Corps as a charter member on August 24, 1885, has been accorded his own chapter in this treatise. His undisputed right to be listed with famous firefighters is hereby recognized; readers desiring to know more about him are now directed to the Chapter entitled: "Captain Blood of the Brigade."

"CAP" SMART

Just a' wee Doch 'n Doris

I HAD A PRETTY SILVER DIME
AS PRETTY AS COULD BE
THE GROCER SAID I'M JUST IN TIME
THE BUTCHER SAID, NO! IT'S FOR ME
THE LANDLORD RANG THE FRONT DOOR BELL
THE COAL MAN HOLLERED DOWN THE FLUE
I TOLD THEM ALL TO GO TO———
AND BOUGHT THIS CARD FOR YOU.

What of the other nominees? The ranks of the Calgary firemen over the years included a significant number of men with artistic talents and skills and it seemed inevitable that the amazing M. S. Carter — better known as Ted Carter — whose creative distinctions included sculpture, music, poetry, inventions, painting and the making of model ships and steam engines, would come to mind.

This native son was born in Calgary in 1926 and was a CFD member for 26 years. He might have been an active fireman in 1985 when the Calgary Department celebrates its 100th birthday had it not been for a motorcycle accident that resulted in serious head injuries. At that point he chose early retirement and the better opportunity to pursue his many hobbies.

In the late years of the Great Depression, this teenager was becoming a handyman in a tire repair shop, then a truck driver and still later a mortician's assistant. He admitted that working at an undertaker's parlor gave him an unusual chance to study human anatomy which helped him in later years as a sculptor and painter.

Then, after the onset of World War II, the versatile Carter became a cook on a naval ship in the North Atlantic. Back in Calgary at war's end, he worked as a City Transit bus driver and then as a fireman. In the latter role he rose to the rank of Captain and might have gone higher if it had not been for the accident.

Being a child of the depression years and busy making a living, he was rather late in giving expression to his ample creativity. One of the earliest demonstrations of his talent was in the co-operative effort that produced a life-size statue of a firefighter holding a child rescued from a burning building. Unveiled in 1967, it was the Calgary firefighters' contribution to Canada's Centennial of Confederation and stands today at the Fire Department's headquarters.

The idea of a Centennial year statue was born at a morning coffee session and four or five firemen friends agreed to help if Carter would take the lead and tell them what to do. The statue began with a wood frame overlaid with screen to hold the plaster. In its early stages, the work of art produced many laughs but after the recognizable shapes of fireman and child emerged and were patiently refined by Carter, the levity turned to admiration. Carter said: "We take humble pride in presenting him as a tribute to the pioneer firemen, the memory of whom inspired the undertaking.

In the meantime, Carter was painting murals, making a room-size replica of the ill-fated steamship, Titanic, and a model engine that would run on its own steam. When the Carter children wanted a toy train,

Dad made one big enough to carry them, also an engine to pull the cars and a backyard railroad to accommodate the train. Bringing no less attention was a small edition of the Sailing Ship, Nonsuch that carried the first shipment of furs from Hudson's Bay to England, resulting in the formation of the Hudson's Bay Company in 1670.

The model of that famous ship, along with models of a Canadian beaver and a totem pole served as patterns for novel 25-ounce whiskey bottles adopted by certain Canadian distillers and sold widely. So popular were the Carter bottles that many non-drinkers were buying the whiskey expressly to obtain the bottles as collectors items.

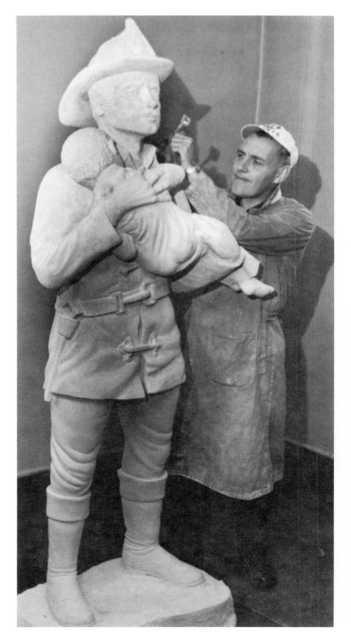

Ted Carter working on statue.

Members who created the statue as a 1967 Centennial Project: G. Coninx, R. Schmidt, Capt. E. Dingley, J. Stewart, M. Carter. This statue is dedicated to the members of the City of Calgary Fire Department who have retired or who have died in service.

Sculpture created by M. Carter for Calgary Firefighters Credit Union.

Some of Ted Carter's Training Sketches

Use Oakum, Steam, or a Torch to thaw out appliances, not a "Hammer or Spanner".

Said officer Drisden, with a voice rich with wisdom:
"All this weather touches, 'It Freezes', So go easy, damn 'er,
Lay off of the hammer. It's hard on the Wye's and siameses."

Fireman Ben, and a couple of men about boating had plenty to learn. They cried with dismay as they swam through the spray, NEVER ANCHOR A BOAT BY THE STERN.

Said officer Hannick.
"The pump driver's panicked"
We'd best all make for the street,
It's not that I care about wet underwear,
"But I've had my bath for this week."

Senior man Sam was a cautious man. He'd already had a few scares. He said with concern, "These rookies will learn". But until then, I'll use the stairs.

Firemen had to be versatile. There was no better example of versatility than Ted Carter's career and creative talents. But Old No. 1 Fire Hall at 6th Avenue and 1st Street, S.E., saw creative art expressing itself in various ways. Soon after that Hall was occupied and a big basement room was fitted as a kitchen, Fireman Bud Fisher undertook to decorate all four walls with murals depicting both Old World and New World scenes. Unfortunately, by their location, the paintings were scarcely known to the public and not appreciated. But 70 years later, the pictures were still there, just as Fisher left them, holding surprise for the few citizens who happened to venture into the old Hall's dungeon-like regions.

Wall Paintings in basement of Old No. 1 Station 6 Ave. and 1 St. S.E. Done by H. (Bud) Fisher.

James Yeates when stationed at the same Hall created the outside basin and fountain that won special fame through the sculptured figures that were added later. Yeates was responsible for the likeness of a fireman shaped in lead for the top position on the fountain and, later, Frank Markle who gained earlier experience in the art of casting metal at the Riverside Ironworks in Calgary, embarked upon the task of making a series of aluminum elephants to stand on the circular rim of the basin.

Markle was a member of the CFD from 1934 until 1971 and the animal figures in salvage aluminum were made about 1945. The elephants were not big, about eight inches tall but expertly turned. When the artistic fellow had enough scrap aluminum to serve his purpose, he obtained permission to use the Riverside Ironworks furnaces and molding sand and there he turned out the famous elephants.

But the much-admired aluminum figures were vulnerable, even though they were fastened to the concrete base of the fountain, and it took a night pirate with a truck only a few minutes to pry the elephants loose and make away with them.

Harry B. Wilson who came from Cooksville, Ontario, in 1889, joined the volunteer CFD seven years later and remained in the service for the next 37 years. At the end of that period it was said of him that he had watched the Department's March of Progress from almost every possible angle, making him one of the best informed persons in the profession.

At the time Wilson joined the Department, Hugh McClelland was the Chief and James Smart was the secretary. Two years later, Smart was elected to become Chief and Harry Wilson succeeded him as secretary.

Firemen in the years prior to 1909 when all workers were placed on a full-time, fully paid basis, had to have other jobs or professions in order to sustain themselves and Wilson's principal livelihood was in the composing room of the Calgary Herald where he worked intermittently for 14 years. Among other firemen working at the Herald in the same years was M. C. Costello who became Mayor of Calgary. Like all the volunteer firefighters, these men were permitted to drop other work at the sound of a fire signal and rush away to the scene of trouble. Employers had to

James Yeates fountain.

be patient. It happened many times when the Herald was late in being delivered that customers murmured almost instinctively: "Whose house or building is burning this time?"

After fighting some of the hottest fires in Calgary's early history and becoming a full time fireman, Wilson was drawn into specialization in Fire Department mechanics and electricity. After being the Chief Mechanic and Electrician, he was appointed to become Calgary's first Superintendent of Alarms. Except for the few years in which Mr. Wilson was overseas in mechanical transport during the First World War, the important work of extending and improving the fire alarm system was uninterrupted until his retirement in 1933.

L. to R.: J. Reinders, H. Wilson, V. Newhall, Chief J. Shelley.

Ontario-born Neil McLaughlin, with the courage of his clansmen ancestors and the muscle of a wrestler, won the right to a place of distinction mainly by his simple and unfailing popularity both within and beyond the ranks of the firemen over 37 years.

Having joined the CFD in 1893 — 16 years before the first motorized apparatus was installed — his specialty was in handling horses while scorning gasoline motors. He was the last man to drive the big ladder wagon and its three-horse team. His skill in breaking, training and driving helped to account for the fine reputation for performance enjoyed by the CFD horses.

In coming to Calgary in 1890 and bringing horses, cattle and machinery from his birthplace of Princeville, Ontario, McLaughlin's intention was to farm at Red Deer Lake, on the town's southwest. But "the best laid schemes O' mice an' men gang aft agley," and before settling down to farm, an opportunity to join the Volunteer Fire Brigade in 1893 resulted in delay and then abandonment of the farming enterprise.

Firefighting instead of farming became his chosen career and as early as 1898 he was speaking out on behalf of his fellow firemen. A letter on Fire Department stationary, dated February 8, 1898, survives to show McLaughlin and Julian Smart petitioning jointly for better wages. Addressing the Mayor and Aldermen, it wastes no time or words in coming to the point: "Gentlemen: We hereby make application for an increase in salary to $50 per month as we consider the wages to be small when a man is supposed to be on duty continually."[1]

On the playing field, soccer and tug-of-war were McLaughlin's best sports and as an individual contestant, his chief fame was in that ancient Scottish test of strength, "the tossing of the caber." About as often as the competition of heaving that pine log was included in the annual sports event at Calgary, McLaughlin was the winner and if there had been a National Caber Championship, he'd have won that too, in all probability.

Neil McLaughlin

Between Neil McLaughlin and Cappy Smart there was a fine feeling of respect and friendship. After the two men came to the age of retirement, they continued to see much of each other until separated by death, Cappy passing in 1939 and McLaughlin living to the age of 87 in 1946.

Joe Fitts who joined the CFD as a firemen and motor mechanic in 1916 and remained for 42 years, was among other things, "the anchor man" on the Department's winning tug-of-war team in the years after World War I. When the importance of keeping the department's growing fleet of motor vehicles operational over a period of more than four decades was considered, it would have been easy to see Fitts as "an anchor man" in a completely different capacity.

There were other reasons for remembering him. At 90 years of age in 1983 and blessed with an exceptional memory, he proved to be one of the best sources of information about pioneer firefighters and their equipment. It was his significant fortune to have served under James Smart and seven other Fire Chiefs, namely: Alex Carr, John McKinnon, John Shelley, Perry Brooks, Ross Kinnear, George Skene and Bernard Lemieux.

Joe Fitts.

Born in Rhode Island in 1893, Fitts was 17 years old when the family came to Alberta to farm 12 miles northeast of Strathmore. How then did he qualify to become the Chief Motor Mechanic for the CFD? To Fitts, the answer was quite logical: after inheriting a natural interest in machines, he was growing up on an Alberta farm on which there were a Ford car, an I.H.C. 2-cylinder gasoline tractor and a good workshop. From the age of 10 years, the young fellow's foremost interest was in gasoline engines.

Less than a year after being hired by Cappy Smart for regular firefighting duty at a wage of $69.35 per month, he was being asked to become the Department's Chief Mechanic. In assuming responsibility for the growing number of fire trucks and related machines, Fitts was doing it like a professional. Thereafter, he was repairing motors in the shop at No. 1, and accompanying the Brigade to all city fires and even to all fires in nearby towns and villages from which calls for help were received, to ensure that the Department's pumps and engines did not fail.

When asked at the age of 90 what he would choose as a career if living over again, he replied promptly: "Join the Calgary Fire Department to keep its wheels turning."

W. H. Cushing, Mayor 1900.

Firefighters Who Enrolled in the early Brigade who Became Mayors of the City of Calgary.

J. W. Mitchell, Mayor 1911-12.   M. C. Costello, Mayor 1915.

Mayors of Calgary

1884-5	George Murdoch	1907- 8	A. L. Cameron
1886-7	G. C. King	1909-10	R. R. Jamieson
1888	A. E. Shelton	1911-12	John W. Mitchell
1889	D. W. Marsh	1913-14	H. A. Sinnott
1890	J. D. Lafferty, M.C.	1915-18	M. C. Costello, M.D.
1891	Jas. Reilly	1919-20	R. C. Marshall
1892-3	A. Lucas	1921-22	S. H. Adams
1894-5	W. F. Orr	1923-26	George H. Webster
1896	A. McBridge	1927-29	Fred E. Osborne
1897	W. F. Orr	1930-45	Andrew Davison
1898	A. L. Cameron	1946-49	J. C. Watson
1899	Jas. Reilly	1950-59	D. H. Mckay
1900	W. H. Cushing	1959-63	H. W. Hays
1901	J. S. Mackie	1963-65	J. W. Grant MacEwan
1902-3	Thomas Underwood	1965-69	J. C. Leslie
1904	S. A. Ramsay	1969-77	R. Sykes
1905-6	John Emerson	1977-80	R. Alger
		1980	R. Klein

Outwardly, it appeared that firefighting was conducted in a man's world. True, the active firefighters were men but in searching for important personalities in the CFD community, the patient and heroic and often lonely wives of firemen should not go unnoticed. If they concluded that there was nothing very romantic about being the wives of firemen on duty for 24 hours a day, six days a week, they would have a strong point.

Fortunately, working conditions were changed dramatically and the Calgary wives formed the CFD Ladies' Auxilliary. Its worthy purpose was to promote fraternal relationships while helping in charitable causes. Unfortunately, the Auxilliary did not live very long.

Ladies' Auxiliary Pins.

But in a chapter intended to name a few outstanding and spectacular personalities in firefighting circles, at least one lady — Minnie Smart — the first of her sex to have a direct working connection with the Department, has earned the right to be included.

Being Cappy Smart's daughter would be almost enough distinction in itself but as her father's secretary, she became one of the best known people in the service. She enjoyed working with and for her father and, like him, was dedicated to fire protection and control. Although she did not engage actively on the hose lines, she had her own rubber coat and helmet and was often present at the scenes of fires. When Calgary firemen responded to calls from High River or Aldersyde or Didsbury, Cappy Smart went along and so did Minnie. Moreover, she knew enough about firefighting that she could always find something useful to do.

Minnie Smart had one brother, James "Bud" Smart, who died at the age of 11 years. She had no sisters.

Minnie Smart, Department First Female Secretary.

142

Research in CFD history must confirm the wide range of able and distinctive people who have served over the years, athletes, sculptors, painters, musicians, inventors, entertainers, men who won later prominence in politics, great soldiers and at least one winner of the Victoria Cross in the First World War, Raphael Louis Zengel, commonly known as Ray Zengel. His actual time in the firefighters' uniform was short but he was remembered, very properly, with special pride.

Ray Zengel.

First he won a Military Medal for bravery in a trench raid on his 23rd birthday, November 11, 1917. And then, a short time later, at Vimy Ridge, his actions brought the still higher award. The citation as reported at the time was in these words: "For most conspicuous bravery and devotion to duty when protecting the battalion's right flank. He [Sergeant Zengel] was leading his platoon gallantly forward to the attack but had not gone far when he realized that a gap had occured on his flank and that an enemy machine gun was firing at short range. Grasping the situation, he [Zengel] rushed forward some 200 yards ahead of the platoon, tackled the machine gun emplacement, killed the officer and operator of the gun and dispersed the crew. By his boldness and prompt action, he undoubtedly saved the lives of many of his comrades."[2]

After the War and after a period with the Calgary Fire Department, Mr. Zengel bought land at Rocky Mountain House and farmed there for 43 years, ultimately retiring at Errington, B.C. His death occured at Nanaimo Regional Hospital on February 25, 1977, at the age of 82.

1914-1918 Honor Roll.

Farewell Flag signed by Members of the Department presented to the 82nd Division.

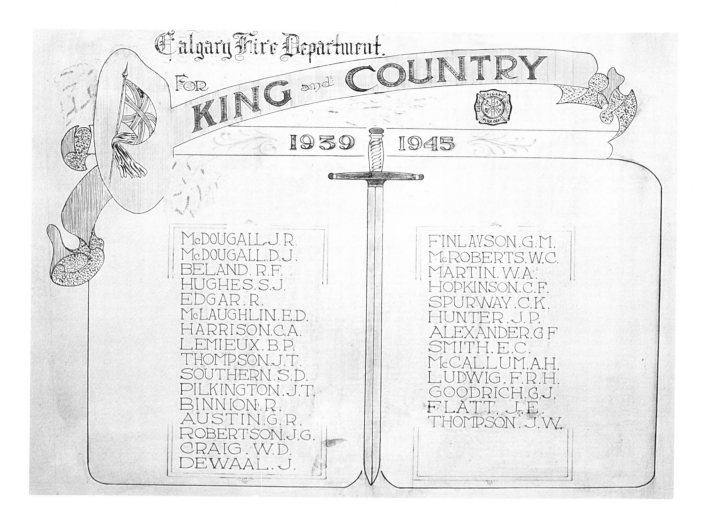

Calgary Fire Department.

FOR KING and COUNTRY

1959   1945

McDOUGALL.J.R.
McDOUGALL.D.J.
BELAND.R.F.
HUGHES.S.J.
EDGAR.R.
McLAUGHLIN.E.D.
HARRISON.C.A.
LEMIEUX.B.P.
THOMPSON.J.T.
SOUTHERN.S.D.
PILKINGTON.J.T.
BINNION.R.
AUSTIN.G.R.
ROBERTSON.J.G.
CRAIG.W.D.
DEWAAL..J.

FINLAYSON.G.M.
McROBERTS.W.C.
MARTIN.W.A.
HOPKINSON.C.F.
SPURWAY.C.K.
HUNTER.J.P.
ALEXANDER.G.F
SMITH.E.C.
McCALLUM.A.H.
LUDWIG.F.R.H.
GOODRICH.G.J.
FLATT.J.E.
THOMPSON.J.W.

144

The C.F.D. Santa Claus Helpers

Just as fires are unpredictable, so the firefighter's working hours will, of necessity, vary from light to heavy and little to much, and enterprising men will search for useful hobbies and sidelines with which to fill spare hours. Of the many useful exercises in which firemen have engaged over the years, one of the most memorable was the unselfish involvement with children's toys, recovering used ones, repairing, repainting and distributing to little people who wanted and needed them at Christmas.

A few spectators, at first, observed critically that the toy business was very foreign to firefighting, but when the full story was told, all thoughts of possible conflict vanished, giving way to public approval and enthusiasm.

It started as a humble Christmas gesture in 1945 when war efforts almost ended toy manufacturing on a commercial scale. As Captain Sid Hughes, George Taylor, Fred Ludwig and Howard Williams engaged in casual conversation at Number 3 Fire Hall in East Calgary, Williams mentioned a certain farm family in which the circumstances of poverty would mar the joy of Christmas. For one thing, the kids would have no toys.

"What say we gather some discard toys from the more fortunate homes and fix them up in our spare time?" one of the men asked. "We might make it a good Christmas for those kids."

The idea was welcomed and an appeal was made to nearby homes where children had outgrown their toys. A teacher at a city school heard about the project and asked her pupils to search their basements and attics for toys no longer needed. The response was excellent and in the words of one of the firemen: "Our quota was away oversubscribed." But because most of the toys required repairs and paint, firemen set about to make them look like new.

As planned, a parcel of these toys, looking as fresh as when they left the stores, was sent to the poverty-stricken family in the country and other toys

The Albertan

CALGARY, ALBERTA, MONDAY, DECEMBER 5, 1949

Toy Hospital Run by Firefighters

Above are four of Santa Claus' helpers (otherwise known as "C" shift of No. 3 Firehall) seen with some of the hundreds of toys they have collected and made as new.

In the group from left to right are: John Bailey, F. R. Ludwig, H. W. Williams and Capt. S. J. Hughes. Two other helpers not in the picture are G. W. Taylor, fireman, and Mrs. H. G. Williams who has been making new frocks for the dolls.

Calgary Firefighters as Santa's Helpers

Home of The Xmas Party.

Santa greeting children.

An anxious moment.

The Xmas party is about to begin.

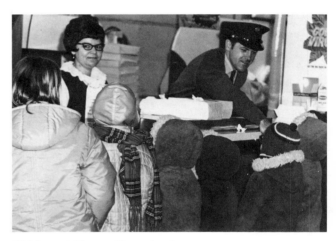

Children picking up Xmas treats.

"And on your way back, stop off and pick up some wrapping paper. And we're out of ribbon too."

146

Thousands of presents being wrapped.

Young fella receives a gift and warm Season's Greetings from D. Tetz.

Santa arrives on antique rig.

P. Baker, master of ceremonies.

Rudolph arrives.

were distributed to needy children in the vicinity of the Fire Hall. Even then, 154 toys remained and, with direction from the City Welfare Department, distribution was extended to more remote districts in the city.

The men responsible knew they could not stop now. In the next year, firemen at two or three other stations adopted toy projects and the Christmas season program grew steadily until 13 of the Calgary Fire Stations were periodically scenes of activity in toy renovation. Now, with operations on a greatly expanded scale, more organization was needed. No longer could firemen collect all the available used toys with their own cars. The cost of repair materials and the purchase of better equipment forced the firemen to appeal for donations. Workshops were fitted with better mechanical aids. A welding outfit was bought, also some power tools. And then, recognizing the size of the program and its importance, the Fire Fighters' Union donated a truck for use in making collections and deliveries of toys.

Denny Craig and son Don presenting gifts to children during Toy Campaign.

As might have been expected, production was changed by specialization. As explained by Calgary-born Fred Parker, Chairman of the Toy Campaign in 1962 and '63, the men at one station specialized in painting, at another in woodwork and still another in metal work. Another group specialized in bicycles, pedal cars and wagons. Hockey and other athletic equipment received specialized attention but when it came to making and repairing clothes for dolls the firemen knew they lacked the expertise required and gladly turned the responsibility over to their wives and womens' organizations which co-operated generously.

The program of 1962, after the years of growth and experience, was being carried out under five project committees. First, there was the committee directing the "Toy Blitz," with students from the Southern Alberta Institute of Technology and Art working on the streets and avenues and resulting in the collection of 30,000 toys. Next there was the

committee organizing a professional hockey game at the Corral for which a new or second hand toy was acceptable for admission. Two truck loads of toys resulted.

The third committee of firemen conducted what was known as Santa Anonymous and by securing the co-operation of a Calgary Radio Station, saw scores of deposit boxes for the receipt of used toys being placed in Calgary stores. The big containers, constructed to resemble chimneys, were the means of making 3,500 more repairable toys available.

Then on the suggestion and with the help of another committee, a department store furnished a huge gift box for used toys, and gave the assurance

Gift boxes being filled up with toys.

that every toy contributed entitled its donor to a reduction of 10 per cent on the purchase of a new toy. Another 500 used toys were recovered for the firemens' work shops this way. And finally, school teachers repeated the invitation to pupils to bring toys no longer in use to school to be forwarded to the firefighter repairmen.

Altogether, the collections ran to 75,000 toys. Not all the toys, understandably, were repairable but from the great stacks of contributions, over 12,000 items were made attractive and in many cases lovable.

Again, the names of families in which need warranted charity, were obtained from the Calgary Council of Community Services, City and Provincial Welfare organizations and churches. Each gift, wrapped carefully and decorated appropriately, contained not less than three toys and 2,501 boys and girls who faced a bleak Christmas, were the recipients and had the joy of opening parcels.

Collection and distribution methods had to be changed from time to time. In 1956 the Calgary Fire Fighters' Toy Campaign was offered the use of Shell Oil Company Service Stations as receiving depots and the working arrangement was continued for some years. Moreover, distribution of so many Christmas parcels as those of the later years, could present problems for the sponsors but again, the

Toy fund raising float.

gayest colors. Decorated Christmas trees, music, clowns and old Santa himself dressed appropriately in fire engine red, combined to ensure the best Christmas atmosphere. And thanks to big cash contributions from the firemens' own organization and donations from clubs and business firms, there were always enough parcels — wrapped gaily by members of volunteer groups in the city — to ensure that every one of the 3,000 or more boys and girls attending would receive at least one.

Regardless of the changing format, the Firemens' Christmas Program for the enjoyment of needy children had become a well founded tradition. Said to be the largest annual Christmas party in Canada, it was certainly one of the best expressions of the Santa Claus spirit and the firemen had good reason for pride.

public rallied to help. In 1962, that final operation was scheduled for the Sunday immediately prior to Christmas Day and truck owners, citizens with cars, citizens without cars and firemen in uniform donated their time and completed delivery in short order. Fifty-four motor vehicles — including some from bread, milk and cartage companies — were counted. And 86 Calgary firemen in uniform assisted where their services were needed.

One of the organizing firemen admitted that he had not been in bed for three days but he was not complaining. His reward — his only reward — was in seeing the thousands of gift-wrapped articles — everything from tin whistles to bicycles — going out to make Christmas a happier time for the little people. He wasn't boasting but he admitted in a whisper that if the kids were happier, he was too.

Instead of disappearing like many institutions suffering from declining enthusiasm, the Calgary Fire Fighters' Christmas Program on behalf of needy kids was still flourishing 40 years after its inception — but in a different form. Because of the so called "Plastic Revolution," the new toys coming on the market and later collected as second hand articles were not repairable like the old ones and the remaking and repair of damaged toys had to be suspended. More funds were then needed for the purchase of new toys.

But the men responsible knew they should not stop. They might change but not stop. Beginning as part of the Firemens' Centennial Year project in 1967, permission was obtained to use the Calgary Stampede Corral and it became the setting for an annual Christmas rally on a monster scale. At the same time, No. 11 Fire Hall at 55th Avenue and 4th Street, S.W., having a spacious basement for storage, became the working headquarters and the project climax came on the last Saturday before Christmas when the Corral was presented in its

Repairing of toys at No. 4 Station: B. Beecher, J. Jack.

[1] McLaughlin, Neil, and Smart, Julian, Letter to Mayor and Aldermen of Calgary. Feb. 8, 1898. (Letter in CFD archives)
[2] London Gazette, Sept. 27, 1918.

The Calgary Fire Fighter's Toy Associa[tion]

wish to thank the following for their support and co-operation in bringing the "Christmas Spirit" to those less fortunate.

A total of 2,119 children were recipients of over 8,000 toys
and 1,903 boys and girls attended the mammoth party held
in the Stampede Corral December 21st.

Calgary Gyro Club
CKXL "Santa Anonymous"
Foothills Wrestling
Hubago Club
Desk & Derrick Club
Pillsbury Mills
Royal Bank
Fire Ladies Bowling
Hudson's Bay
T. Eaton's
Federated Car Clubs
South Calgary Kindergarden
Elbow Park Kindergarden
Greenview Nurseries
Industrial Acceptance
Woodward's
Montreal Trust
Barber Ellis
105 Cu...

R.E.A.C.T.
Calgary Zoo
Jack Jones
Don Canning
The "Caribs"
"Buckshot"
Wynne Hanson
Jan Fulton Dancers
Ogston Kids
Spady Kids
Father Lacombe Staff
Mrs. W. H. Laycock
Christmas Bureau
Beta Sigma Phi
Beta

Exhibition & Stam...
Senger Photo &...
Compac Commercia...
Calgary Milk F...
Canada Saf...
E. T. Mar...
Scott Nationa...
Island Mill...
CFCN Radi...
CF...

The Cosmopolitan Clubs of Calgary

in co-operation with the

Calgary Fire Department
TOY CAMPAIGN

Offer

HALLOWE'EN
COSMO-
TREATS

...ER 17-30, 19...

Contests, Clowns, Displays

Fire Department To Reviv City Fir
Annual Demonstration Sho Open T

The Calgary fire department
will stage a demonstration show
Sept. 11, 7 p.m., at Mewata
Park.

The display, once an annual
event, will be presented for the
first time in 14 years. Rescue
methods, fire - fighting techniques and new and old equipment will be shown.

Firemen will battle a mock
fire in a specially - constructed
platform and demonstrate rope
and stretcher rescue methods
from a scaffold.

Teams from various city fire
halls will compete in the hose-
laying contest and clowns will
hold a water fight.

IMPROVE METHODS

William Phillips, rescue officer, said after a practice session:

"Every day a new group is

brought to the training g. Christmas — from midr
at 9th Ave. and 20th St. Monday — is 2,208 hours a
to improve rescue methods That's about an hour
hose-laying times. every Calgary child who

"The department has m every Calgary child unless yo
doing drills every day but t be disappointed unless yo
competition becomes keen Calgary firemen laun
when they look forward to some annual St. Nick drive
thing like this demonstration,' pairable toys October
Mr. Phillips said. During the next

"When they aren't training, half months the toys
...d ...tures or are out reconditioned and
...... to the c

Merry Christmas for All

More Toys Needed
For City Children

City firemen are waging an children wiped out their toy
11th-hour campaign to find a toy supply.
for every Calgary child this Despite this, toys were de-
Christmas. livered to 2,100 children during
The firemen thought they had the weekend.
situation under control but a Toys are needed for all age
into the weekend but a groups from one to 12 years.
...inute list of 1,100 needy A pick-up can be arranged by
phoning 266-6937.

SANTA'S HELPERS. Firemen today readied giant piles of toys (20,000 of them) for del
1,000 city homes Sunday. The deliveries, which will start early Sunday morning, will continu
until the local fire fighters have placed toys under the tree of every unfortunate family on th
deliveries, like the rest of the campaign, will be entirely voluntary, and at the expense of the fire
fireman Phil Paulson, left, and Capt. Ted Greengrove, head of the ca... ...gn, ready a pile of lar
from No. 11 hall in Manchester.

Firemen at No. 11 Fire-Hall, 55th Ave.
and 4th St. S.W., help a delivery man
load his truck. More than 2,000 city
children were given toys as a result of

the city fire department's annua
mas toy campaign. The toy dr
begun just after the Second Wor
— Walter Petrig

Firemen Are All Set To Go
With Carloads Of Yule Cheer

▶ ...ART S...
...The del
...at 9 a...
...will gath
fire halls
of toys w
deliveries
will be
morning.
Toys fo

Santa Rides a Bread Tru
As Firemen Make Roun

DELIVERIES BEGIN. Calgary firemen smile Sunday morning as they check their stock of toys for 367 needy families in the city. Here (left to right) firemen Brian Garraway; Fred Parker, toy campaign chairman and Maurice Simonin, pack toys prior to delivery. About 25 firemen and many volunteer workers delivered about 2,300 toys with two fire trucks during the day before their supply ran short.

Firemen Still Seek 1,500 Gifts To Brighten Yule For Needy

The annual firemen's toy campaign needs 1,500 more toys in order to brighten Christmas for all of the 367 needy families on their ___

buy more toys so we can provide for all the families.

"We can't disappoint children," he said ___

300 gifts if we plan to give to every family and their children," he said

The Western Farm Scene

Firemen and Toys Go Together In Calgary Christmas Project

By Grant MacEwan

Firefighters to Be Santa to 750 Families

Santa's helpers, the firefighters of the Calgary Fire Department, will be delivering more than 10,000 gifts to 750 needy ___ies in the city Sunday ___
mammoth job ___
___ther at ___
___here ___

There are so many ___ people calling up s___ have toys for ___ almost impossib___ with the colle___ of teenage ___ selves the ___ ups.

_rive

dwork and wa
airs bicycles and
l stores recondi
and No. 13 distri

nt to poverty-
_l days

Christmas Campaign

Wanted -- 60,000 Toys

What d___ ___remen want for Christm___
Fewer ___
The ___
Camp___
men ___
and ___
fi___
h___

other stations, and now 11 out of 13 fire halls work on the toy campaign, involving some 250 out of 402 Calgary firefighters. The work is done between ___se duty and drills. And ___ between 50,000 to ___ the smallest ___ ___ ___

er says presents for girls in this age bracket are very difficult to come by) and all other toys that are being discarded.

EDDED WHEA

AROUND CALGARY

Calgary fire department will hold a demonstration in Mewata Stadium Sept. 11 at 7 p.m. Firemen will demonstrate six fire fighting techniques including ladder work, display by clowns and use of foam and rescue apparatus. A water fight, display by ___ an exhibition of old time apparatus will touches.
Provide the lighter ___

_l toys ___n they rived ___ened says ___ s have ar-
containin_
of broken plum_, fixtures, dis-
carded shoes, even adult type worn out pots and pans — none of which can be used, and must be carted away to the nearest dump.

Mr. Parker pays tribute to the people who pitch in and help the campaign. The ladies of the Golden Age Club dress the dolls, as do several individual women, "when the dolls come back for delivery at Christmas they have wardrobes that would do credit to a princess."

C 80-598 ALBERTA

YS ARRIVE. Another truck-load of toys for the fire de___ above being unloaded by two workers in the campaign. The ___mber 10,000 are repaired when possible and given to needy ___. In the above photograph fireman Norman Lockwood assists fireman ___ki, right, unload a box of toys at campaign headquarters in No. 4 firehall. ___ want to distribute 20,000 toys to more than 2,000 families this year.

_emen Have Hands Full

_ending Toys For Christmas

helpers in Calgary —
_of the fire department—
_r hands full with toys
_ll decorate Christmas
_many unfortunate chil-
_year.

the occasional piece for repair purposes.
The main workshop and marshalling point is at No. 4 firehall, in northeast Calgary, where truck loads of toys are brought in at the ___ ___ ___

Last year 15,000 toys were del_ered to 1,800 families by the smol_ eaters.

40,000 COLLECTION
To get their desired objective 20,000 repairable toys for deliver_ ___

FIREFIGHTER Larry Schumaker wields a crescent wrench on the wheel of a toy truck that will help to make some small moppet's Christmas merry.

21st Annual Toy Campaign. L-R: T. Cuthbert, Mayor G. MacEwan, Chief C. Harrison, F. Parker.

L-R: J. Bailey, H. Anderson, E. Wilson, repairing toys.

Fun And Sentiment At The Fire Hall

It was to be expected that men with varying spells of idle time would make their own fun and create their own humor. The Fire Hall humor was not necessarily for all ears but it would rate high in originality. The stories told represented different combinations of fact and fiction but probably did injury to nobody.

No doubt it was just such a hybrid story that was told about an urgent telephone call received from a lady presumed to be an elderly spinster. She reported excitedly that a strange man was attempting to enter her second floor window. Trying to be helpful, the operator at the Fire Hall switchboard interrupted to say: "Madam, this is the Fire Department and you should be calling the City Police. I will give you the police number."

To which the lady replied, impatiently: "I don't want the police. I want the Fire Department because this man needs a longer ladder."

Unfortunately, nobody was able to tell or willing to tell if the lady's earnest wish for a longer ladder was granted. When questioned about the story, one of the members of the CFD, with twinkle in his eye, said his friends in the service would prefer to avoid becoming involved in events like this because it would be most embarrassing if the man at the window was found to be one of the firefighters.

When older members and pensioners of the Department said: "I remember," authors and others should have known to reach for pens and paper. One with a good memory and good sense of humor, former District Chief, C. F. Hopkinson, told of another emergency call that made it extremely difficult for him and the men with him to keep straight faces. As he related the episode, the call brought the rescue van and command car to the scene but the backyard was already crowded with spectators, necessitating a message for police officers to exercise crowd control.

The unfortunate victim of circumstances was a very large lady who, upon leaving her house at an earlier hour, had inadvertantly locked herself out without a key. On returning, she looked in vain for a means of re-entry and finally decided to try the milk chute. Obviously, the decision was made without proper consideration of her own generous proportions in relation to the limitations of the chute. But she was determined and started in, head first. Her head passed through without difficulty and shoulders and breasts passed with difficulty. But when she tried to bring her hips through, she discovered impossibility and she was stuck with head, shoulders and "bountiful bosoms" on the inside, and hips and posterior on the outside. She could move neither forward nor backward.

It was a delicate situation and more firemen were needed. The first objective was to gain entrance to the inside of the house but it was noticed that an upstairs bathroom window was partly open and the slimmest fireman in the service was able to squeeze through from a ladder and unlock a door. With two

Captains present, one of them, with helpers, took charge of operations on the inside and the other on the outside, with strategy being coordinated by means of a "walkie-talkie." An ambulance stretcher was in readiness if needed and the order was given to procede gently with the removal.

The lady was to be withdrawn by pulling on her clothes to prevent garments from bunching and making new obstacles. The outside crew did the pulling but the insiders had the bigger task, having to support the lady's arms and head and lift the breasts to ease them over the inside sill. The onlookers grew more numerous but the work, according to Mr. Hopkinson, advanced smoothly and ultimate release brought a cheer of triumph from the spectators. The lady made a hasty retreat into the house, with no lasting ills except embarrassment.

Some of the Fire Hall fun and humor was planned, some unplanned. One fireman's embarrassment from responding to an alarm at a midnight hour without trousers may have been planned by mischievous colleagues but if it was, the planners were never identified. The fireman residing at the Hall made the usual bedtime preparations for rapid entry into his clothes in case of a night time alarm but when the alarm did sound on this night and he sprang to the call of duty, he couldn't find his trousers. He knew the fire truck would not wait and it would not do to let it depart without him. The decision could not be delayed. He pulled on his rubber boots and helmet and dashed out to slide down the pole and ride away to the fire, pantless. Fortunately, midnight fires never did attract many spectators and fellow firefighters seemed to enjoy their co-worker's dilemma.

One of the well known Fire Chiefs in the years when Chiefs maintained sleeping quarters at the Fire Hall, had a similar experience. This Chief who was remembered as a good leader, wore a wig and did not wish to be seen without it. Nor did he wish to make his wig a subject for needless conversation and entertainment.

Faithfully, upon retirement at bedtime, he would set out his night hitch and other items of clothing and carefully place his wig inside the fireman's helmet so that both could be placed on his head with a single stroke, all to permit the fastest possible act of dressing in the event of an alarm. But even the Chief was not immune to Fire Hall pranks and during the night in question when most people were sound asleep, somebody tampered with the wig and reversed its position in the helmet.

Sure enough, there was a nighttime alarm and the Chief, just about half awake pulled on the various articles of clothing, including the helmet, and was speeding away to the fire before he realized that his wig was in a backward position on his head, with the long hair that normally hung at the back of his neck, hanging now over his eyes. He had no intention of drawing needless attention to his wig by changing its position in public or in the presence of his men and, being a good fireman, he went about his duty as usual, notwithstanding the long false hair hanging over his eyes.

The Fire Hall shenanigans were, for the most part, directed at individuals who were guilty of perpetrating their own practical jokes and the new men who brought an annoying amount of arrogance and conceit with them. Just as upper class University students believed that freshmen should be humbled by the traditional process of initiation, so the older residents at the Fire Hall believed the newcomers to the force should be given a chance to prove their courage and ability to take a joke.

Many of the pranks at No. 1 Fire Hall were sparked by a relatively harmless electrical device consisting of four dry batteries and an ignition coil from an early Ford car, all carefully wired together to deliver a somewhat amplified shock to the unsuspecting person believed guilty of pomposity. The "executioner" in most instances was fun-loving William Hamilton, distinguished member of the Calgary Firefighters' famous clown team.

L-R: W. Hamilton, H. Tucker, H. Smith.

154

A salute to Division Chief (retired) Bill Hamilton.

Hamilton knew how to thread a mattress with fine wires and suspend the batteries and coil on the under side of the bed, with an inconspicuous wire extension to a switch concealed in his own bed. The moment for action would come shortly after the lights were turned out at 11 p.m. and the outcome was generally easy to forecast. With an undignified leap from his bed, the victim would shriek and stumble over his rubber boots as he hit the floor.

One of the newcomers to No. 1 Fire Hall, more bombastic than most, was soon marked for a reproving jolt. His bed was beside the radiator and Bill Hamilton offered some friendly advice: "Better move your bed away from that metal radiator because we're getting a lot of night storms just now and you never know when lightning will strike and when it will travel along the metal pipes to that radiator."

The opinionated fellow laughed and said with boastful air: "I'm not afraid of lightning."

Hamilton knew at once that he had a proper customer for his electrical treatment. Along about midnight when another summer storm broke over Calgary and the dormitory was in darkness and tranquillity, Hamilton, instead of sleeping, was waiting for the next big flash of lightning. When it struck, casting an instant of midday light over the region, he immediately closed the switch and watched through the gloom as the occupant of the bed beside the radiator sprang as if blasted from his blankets, shouting: "I'm struck by lightning! I'll never sleep near a radiator again."

But, said Joe Fitts, "we were like one big family, constantly playing tricks on each other. Occasionally somebody thought the joke was being carried too far, as in the case of Harry Wilson who always hung his fire coat on a one-post hall rack. A friendly fireman with no evil intentions buckled the coat around the post and walked away. When the next fire alarm was sounded, the unsuspecting Harry was seen struggling to take the coat off the clothes stand and puzzled because the piece of furniture wanted to come too.

"He was pretty mad," Fitts said, "and offered to fight the man who did it."[1] But the culprit didn't identify himself and the victim didn't look very hard for him and there was no lasting animosity.

Fitts, who looked back upon 42 years in the CFD service, snickered again when recounting Jack Carey's error in leaving a pair of dirty trousers to soak in a tub of water to which a pinch of lye had been added "to cut the grease." The lye might have been useful but the fireman's mistake was in leaving the can of lye beside the tub and almost every fireman going by paused to sprinkle a bit more lye on the soaking garments. "When Jack went to recover his trousers, all that remained were the shreds."

There were the serious tragedies that brought genuine sorrow to the Fire Hall community as there were, also, the minor accidents about which there was a humorous side. When Fitts, as Chief Motor Mechanic, was working on a crankshaft bearing and rotating the shaft back and forth — thereby causing the exposed mooring gears to turn — one of the young firemen stopped to enquire about what was going on. Before Fitts had time to explain, the visitor pointed at the moving gears and in misjudging the distance, he suffered the misfortune of having the end of his pointing finger painfully crushed off.

That wasn't funny but next day while Fitts was engaged with exactly the same task, the young fireman came again with a friend and stopped to point out how the accident had occurred. Again he pointed at the gears and again he misjudged the distance. But this time, with a change of pointing finger, he was more lucky; as the story was told, he didn't actually lose the point of another finger but came away with lubricating grease on it. "If I hadn't stopped turning the shaft," said Fitts, "he would have lost the second fingertip in two days."

A fireman had to feel very bold to play a trick on one of the Smarts, of whom there were five at the CFD at one time — the Chief, brothers Julian, Jack, Tom and, daughter, Minnie. But nobody was really immune to pranks and the Chief on an April Fool's day came to his office to find one of the fire horses tied to the desk. Mercifully, he did not attempt to find the offender. And daughter, Minnie, when working as her father's secretary, found on another occasion, her pet English bulldog with its rear end painted a bright fire engine red.

Cappy Smart enjoyed fun as much as anybody but he could be tough when he disapproved. When he found two of his men at No. 1 Fire Hall engaged in a serious fistfight, he stepped in and separated them, then ordered them to pay penalty by proceeding at once to the Fire Hall bell tower together and not to come down until they had completed painting it, all of it. The idea was that in so doing, they would learn something about working together.

Minnie's bulldog.

But back of all the fun and mischief were the clear evidences of loyalty and sentiment. The men would work overtime to make their famous Firefighters' Clown team available for parades and club programs whenever requested, with payments — if any — going to the Department's charity fund. Proudly they played baseball, soccer, hockey and curling on CFD teams and won high honors. Faithfully they supported their Christmas Toy Campaign and patiently flooded rinks for junior hockey and kids' skating, and operated Saturday morning "barbershops" at several of the Fire Halls for free haircuts for children whose parents didn't find it easy to pay the regular barber fees; that was a service of which the general public heard little or nothing.

With typical sentimental fervor, the firemen remembered those of the service who volunteered for war duty in two World Wars, some of whom did not return, some of whom returned with wounds and disabilities.

They formed a fierce enthusiasm for the aging Fire Hall No. 1 at the corner of 6th Avenue and 1st St. S.E., when its usefulness appeared to have ended and it was threatened with demolition. And the same sort of loyalty could be recognized for the two old bells that seemed to symbolize the dramatic history of the Department.

The story of the bells — the big one that rests proudly at the entrance to the new No. 1 Fire Hall and the smaller one enjoying its retirement at Heritage Park in Calgary — did not escape some confusion and some contradictions by writers. Unfortunately the old bells could not recite their own story but there is now the best of reason for believing that the smaller bell now at Heritage Park, was the first to hang in the tower over Calgary's first Fire Hall on McIntyre Avenue, built in 1887. There it pealed its message to volunteer firemen and others by means of clappers driven by suspended weights.

But as the Calgary community grew, people living in outlying parts were unable to hear the sound of the bell and on the occasion of one serious fire, half of the volunteer firemen did not respond because they missed the call. The Mayor and aldermen agreed that this failure had to be corrected and the much bigger, 1300-pound bell now at No. 1 Fire Hall was ordered and hung.

The smaller bell, at this point, might have been lost. It wasn't. Speaking of it, the authors of the Heritage Park Story state: "In 1948 Fire Chief John T. Shelley presented the bell to the Zoological Society which in turn presented it to Heritage Park in 1965 to remind us of pioneer days when the clang of the bell alerted the whole community to the danger of fire."[2]

In the meantime, the big bell was moved to the new Fire Hall at 6th Ave. and 1st St., S.E. in 1911 where it remained until removed in 1946 because of the aging and weakening belfry. By that time it had endeared itself to the Calgary people and was not in danger of being lost.

The two bells that once sounded the warnings of fire and rang on more cheerful occasions like the beginning of a new year, are now and for all time to come, among Calgary's most prized treasures, symbolizing the progress, courage, fun and sentiment of yesteryears and the hope for tomorrow.

Bell at Heritage Park.

Bell at No. 1 Station 5 Ave. and 1st St. S.E.

Heritage Park Days, 1975. G. Young, C. Adair, G. Caron, J. Ingram, B. Scott, B. Zoback, L. Thompson, B. Dancy (in water).

Training crews having a break, awaiting the challenge.

Tug of war teams.

Water fight.

Tug of War, Fire versus city Police.

It's not connected.

157

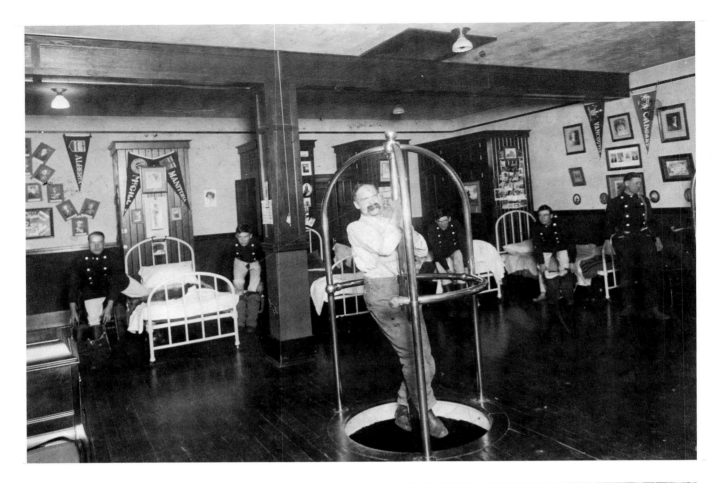

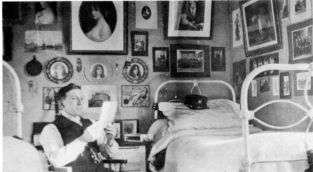

Early Scenes Around The Fire Stations

Note: The Interior Decorating

What Of Firefighting Tomorrow?

When conversation turns to the spectacular changes in firefighting techniques between 1885 and 1985, questions are likely to arise: What next? What will be the fireman's position in 1995 and 2085?

None but prophets can answer but it is everybody's right to speculate about changes. It seems safe to say that some of the demands upon the public firefighters will remain without change. The need for fire prevention education, for example, will continue to be important. Unless human nature can be improved, the work of arsonists will continue to add to the firefighters' responsibilities and unless carelessness in homes and business premises can be corrected, the people who man the fire departments will still be on 24-hours-per-day call.

In some other branches of the service, however, changes will occur, some of them sweeping in impact. Certainly, members of Calgary's Hook, Ladder and Bucket Corps, working on a voluntary basis from the time of their organization on August 24, 1885, could not have foreseen a fully motorized fire brigade being achieved in less than the years of an average span of human life. Nor could they have anticipated the community changes that would bring

Airport crash stand-by.

Water rescue.

Airport firefighting.

all ambulance services to the Fire Department and place the main city reliance upon trained firemen for water rescue.

The firefighters of a hundred years ago would not have envisioned the new and specialized tasks that would fall to Calgary firemen at the airport. They would not see and would not have understood if they had seen the full meaning of the newspaper headlines of 79 years later: "McCall [Airfield] Fire Crews Among The Best Of Kind."[1] It meant, of course, that special problems existed where fires fed by gasoline and other aircraft fuel could occur and where firemen had to be ready to deal with the savage blazes from the burning fuselage of a downed aircraft. The background fact in this news report was that the City of Calgary took over the firefighting responsibilities at McCall Field in 1962 and retained them when the Calgary facility became the International Airport. Gradually, members of the Fire Hall at the Airport came to be seen as specialists among specialists, ready to fight fires with foam and chemicals as well as water, often far from a hydrant.

But in considering the new challenges in firefighting in the years ahead, nobody should overlook or discount the current dangers and difficulties cre-

Airport mock up training.

PWA Flight 501 Boeing 737, March 22, 1984.

ated by the modern city structures of skyscraper proportions. The very thought of fire at their higher levels brought some observers to refer to them as "highrise horrors." As everybody agrees, such buildings must have nothing less than the best "built-in" safeguards such as fire resistant construction, smoke detectors, hand extinguishers and automatic sprinklers. Important as such provisions might be, they are no guarantee of safety, especially at floor levels far beyond the reach of the best ladder equipment. Moreover, elevators and stairways may hold their own dangers in times of fire. What then does the future hold for those unfortunate people who may be trapped above the reach of the best ladders at the time of writing or at levels beyond the 15th or 16th floor? Ways of relieving such high level threats and dangers will be found and the art of firefighting will triumph again. Meanwhile, the situation invites the best in imagination and inventiveness and time is short.

Calgary, to the time of writing, has been fortunate in escaping a serious fire in one of its many highrise buildings. But there is never a guarantee that such good fortune will last. Speaking in early 1976, a representative of the Fire Department said: "It's not a question of if; it's a question of when it's going to happen."[2]

Citizens had a scary warning when a fire occurred at the Calgary Tower, forcing dinner guests at the high level restaurant to walk down the 762 steps to the street. The fire did damage amounting to $50,000 but apparently did not create enough heat to trigger the automatic sprinkler system and, in the excitement of the moment, nobody thought of manually activating the system.

One suggestion offered as a solution to the rescue problem in highrise buildings and likely to be heard again: "Insist upon proper landing pads on the roofs of all high buildings for the use of helicopters in evacuating residents in the event of fire." Very likely, residents could on occasions be removed from rooftops by this means but there is adequate reason to question the reliability and safety of a helicopter strategy.

Unless a helicopter was kept for exclusive use in rescue work, there would be no guarantee of one being available when an emergency arose and nobody should overlook the possible difficulties and dangers in trying to land on a rooftop pad of a city building under fire conditions. Smoke, wind and a strong updraft of hot air from the fire could make for

Highrise rescue training.

Helicopter rescue training.

trouble in getting close to a burning building and double trouble in landing. And with a large number of hysterical people on the roof, desperately eager to gain admittance to the rescue machine, the difficulty of lifting off could be compounded.

The use of the helicopter in highrise rescue remains a possibility but some experienced operators are advising that: "We dare not depend upon it yet, at least not until we must abandon hope of finding something better." Sharing this opinion was a Calgary Fire Department representative, Jack Bell, who, when speaking to a gathering of builders in 1981 declared that the helicopter was still a matter of "last resort" in recovering people from high buildings. He then added: "The best and most practical solution to highrise fires is to provide proper early detection and containment of the flames."[3]

It was increasingly clear by 1980 that firefighters and professional planners would be devoting more of their future to building requirements that would ensure the best degree of safety. Hotels became the main subject of concern and debate. Calgary's Fire Chief, Frank Archer, late in that year, was pointing warningly at the recent MGM Grand Hotel fire in Las Vegas that took 84 lives and calling for legislation that would make the sprinkler system mandatory in all highrise hotels.

Yes, there was some controversy. Owners of hotels without sprinklers were frightened by the anticipated cost of installation in old buildings and one of the owners suggested that smoke detectors would be more practical and more important. His contention was that "smoke detectors save lives while sprinklers protect buildings."[4]

Another hotel man suggested that instead of naming sprinklers as a hotel requirement, it would be better to demand pressurization in all stairwells which have often acted like chimneys when fire occurred. The fans would prevent smoke from entering the stairwells which might otherwise become death traps for people who, in a state of panic, would rush blindly to them when smoke and flames were detected.

If the past is any indication of the future — which it is most likely to be — firefighting techniques will continue to change. It is quite conceivable that some part of urban attack upon fires will be conducted from the air. If such be the case, firefighters will be seen studying aeronautics just as their fellow workers were studying scuba diving so recently to fit themselves for underwater and rescue duties.

The firefighter of tomorrow will direct more sophisticated machines and more effective fire suppressing agents. New chemicals and foam may play bigger parts in the struggle. There are many possibilities and nobody at this time needs to be so reckless as to try to define the new tools. One thing becomes increasingly certain, that the firefighter of tomorrow will need a good educational foundation on which to build a career. He will have a special need for a thorough grounding in chemistry, physics and mathematics. And courses in engineering would bring further benefit. Indeed, the day will come when the candidate for firefighting will not be accepted without a least moderately high academic credentials.

Of course there are many uncertainties about firefighting in tomorrow's world. It would be well, however, to conclude these chapters with a few references to the certainties in the years ahead. The firefighter can be certain that urban society will need him and have a dependant's feeling toward him. And those who turn to him for his expert and courageous help, will want it in a hurry. Nothing is more certain.

The firefighter of tomorrow will certainly need that traditional versatility, a trademark of the profession, perhaps need it more than ever. He should be reminded that he, more than anybody in the public service, must be prepared to confront the disasters that strike without warning, regardless of the dangers. A community stunned by cyclone, flood, fire, explosion or mechanical disaster will look to its Fire Department, expecting help and guidance. With such a trust, the firefighters services must extend beyond the call of duty.

Former Fire Chief W. D. Craig sounded the proper note for the firefighters of tomorrow: "Modern working conditions have changed the role of the firefighter in the community but he continues to play an essential part . . . as he responds to the demands of his occupation in a world where risks and hazards become more severe from year to year and the safety of the people he is expected to protect becomes ever more threatened by the products of modern discoveries and technology. Many times he will go far beyond what is expected of him as he responds to the emergency and routine calls that no other department in the city service is expected or equipped to handle. The role of the fire service will change as it adapts to the needs of the times but it will continue to operate as a department the prime function and dedication of which is to protect life and property."[5]

[1] Fitts, Joe, Recollections, Unpublished, Nov. 18, 1974.
[2] Burns, Vera; Campbell, W. J. and Turner, D. H. L., The Heritage Park Story, p. 26, Printed by Strathmore Standard Newspaper Office, Heritage Park, 1976.
[1] Calgary Herald, April 18, 1964.
[2] Calgary Herald, March 1, 1976.
[3] Calgary Herald, May 15, 1981.
[4] Calgary Herald, Nov. 25, 1980.
[5] Craig, W. D., Recollections and Observations, A contribution to the Centennial record, March 25, 1983.

A Glance At The Future!

by Fire Chief Tom Minhinnett

I am deeply honored by the opportunity to contribute to this book on the history of the Calgary Fire Department. The views or opinions that I express are personal and do not necessarily reflect the philosophies or policies of the City of Calgary or those of such a prestigious author as Dr. MacEwan.

My years of experience with the Calgary Fire Department have taught me that when writing of the future, it is important to do it in the light of events and experience over the past one hundred years.

The book will point up the notable changes that have taken place in the Calgary Fire Department in the past century. They may not differ greatly from changes seen in other Fire Departments but they are changes that touch all of us. Whether of our own making or not, such changes bring problems as well as benefits. An example of an innovation that brought far-reaching problems was in the use of chemicals such as Poly Vinyl Chlorides. Neither as a young firefighter nor later as a young officer could I have foreseen the dangers to which present day firefighters would be exposed.

Dangerous and often toxic by-products are generated when man-made materials are exposed to fire. Many of these by-products are not only dangerous when inhaled but also when absorbed through the skin. The full long-term effect of exposure to these materials may not be known for years to come.

It goes without saying that fire problems and firefighting techniques have undergone spectacular changes. Methods and equipment had to be adapted and modified to fit changing lifestyles. The process of change has even accelerated in recent years. We have, it seems, been exposed to more and more knowledge at a faster and faster rate.

Many of those changes have been effected by men within our Department. One of the truly significant changes has been the reduced hours of work. Men of the original Calgary Fire Department were required to work twenty-four hours a day, seven days a week. A few hours of free time were allowed for the performance of essential domestic duties only. Today's firefighters work a forty-two hour week.

Such a change coupled with the phenomenal growth of the City has tended to dilute the role of the individual and demanded major increases in both training programs and training facilities.

Recent economic downturns inhibited the fulfillment of training objectives but I am confident that we will still be successful in meeting the essential requirements.

Generally speaking, we are moving in the right direction with our fire suppression capabilities. Public education and fire prevention programs, will be re-emphasized in the coming years. A program developed by the National Fire Protection Association entitled "Learn Not To Burn", when used by other Fire Departments, has been effective in not only preventing fires, but in minimizing the effects. All too often we find human error as the cause of fires. These errors are generally related to lack of knowledge on the part of citizens and compounded by failure to be properly aware of existing programs.

I am increasingly concerned about the safety of our firefighters who are or may be exposed to the various by-products of combustion. Our involvement with the various research programs being conducted by groups both in Canada and the United States must continue. "Every" firefighter is trained in the most up-to-date methods of firefighting. He is supplied with the latest in life safety equipment. To preserve his life and to maintain a quality work environment, it is essential that today's firefighters have the benefits of the most modern safety measures.

Calgary's Fire Chiefs
1885-1985

G. Constantine, 1885.

S. Jarret, 1885-1887.

F. Dick, 1887.

E. Rodgers, 1887-1889.

F. Dick, 1889-1892.

J. Wilson, 1893-1897.

H. McClelland, 1897-1898.

J. (Cappy) Smart, 1898-1933.

A. Carr, 1933-1943.

J. MacKinnon, 1943-1945.

J. Shelley, 1945-1950.

P. Brooks, 1950.

R. Kinnear, 1950.

G. Skene, 1951-1954.

B. Lemieux, 1954-1964.

C. Harrison, 1964-1972.

D. Craig, 1972.

D. Jackson, 1972-1979.

F. Archer, 1979-1983.

T. Minhinnett, 1983-.

In the years to come, scientific research will bring still more sophistication in both firefighting tools and methods. A few of the hazards and dangers will hopefully subside with each advance. Perhaps the simple act of pushing a button will one day contain and extinguish fires, saving our members from the punishment of heat and smoke.

Like us, other Fire Departments are pursuing fitness and health programs. We are constantly searching for better ways of improving our standards. Objective research must be carried out continuously.

As in the past, our primary goal will be a reduction in loss of lives and property caused by fire or accident. Department activities such as public education, fire prevention, pre-fire planning, training, maintenance, and research and development should become more visible. They will compliment each other in a well balanced Fire Department and prove essential to the total Fire Protection effort.

The following is a brief review of our Department's activities.

Public Education

To sound an old cliche heard in fire prevention circles, the three principle causes of fire are "men, women and children". Informing people of what they can do to prevent fires from starting is elementary and must be followed by emphasis upon proper procedure in notifying the Fire Department as promptly as possible when fire becomes a reality. Members of the public must be kept constantly aware of how to escape from buildings and how to assist others to escape. This is no small task because people in our society are commonly apathetic toward fire dangers. Too often citizens ignore what everybody should know about life saving measures. Success in reaching the goal of public understanding in fire matters will mean a reduction of the frequency of "nuisance fires" and an overall reduction in the severity of fires. In recent years, built-in fire protection devices have resulted in an increased public awareness but much remains to be accomplished.

Fire Prevention

Identification of potential fires and forces contributing to the spread of fires are proper objectives in Fire Prevention. This calls for a broad range of tasks in property inspecting, code enforcement and validation of building plans. All of these activities are aimed at the removal of conditions that are likely to cause or magnify a fire problem. Fire Prevention is considered to be one of our most important tasks. Unfortunately, it is not interfaced with all elements of the system at all times.

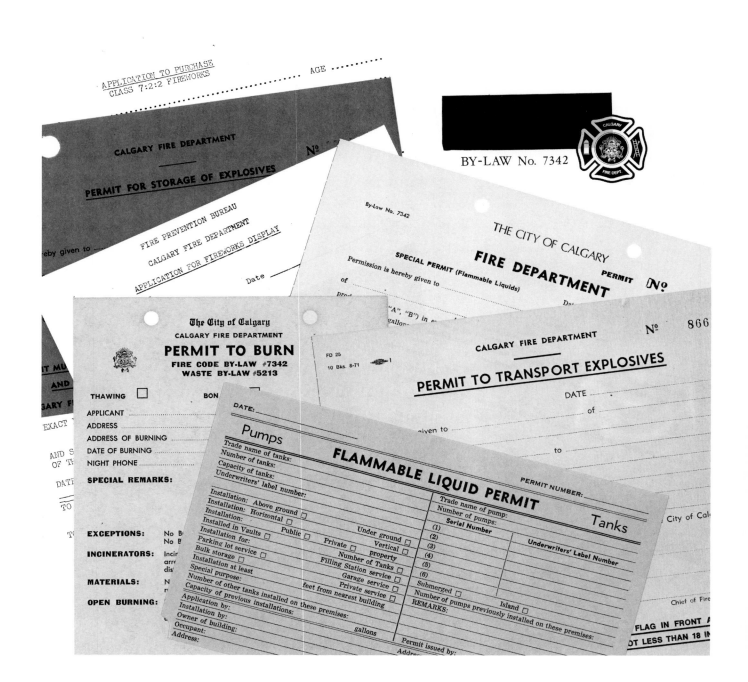

Pre-Fire Planning

Collecting facts and information from other components within our Department for use at an actual emergency is an important part of pre-planning. This information should be assessed in relation to other factors such as manpower, resource allocation, present techniques and equipment to see if problems can be identified before actual emergencies occur. The pre-planning component is extremely important in identifying areas of weakness. The term pre-planning does not mean that each fire can be accurately assessed in advance but it does mean that firefighters will have better information available when faced with the call for immediate action.

Aerial Drill.

High Rise Cover and Book Title.

Maintenance

Maintenance activities on our Department ensure that all our equipment is dependable. It is essential that all apparatus checks, routine maintenance and continuous attention to detail are maintained so that our equipment is ready when needed.

It is vital to the economy of our operation that a preventative maintenance program, designed to increase the longevity of our equipment, was instituted and is to be continued. Maintenance activities take up a significant amount of everyone's time but there is no doubt that it is time well spent.

Disaster Services

The Alberta Disaster Services Act, empowers the City of Calgary to establish a Disaster Services Agency. The Fire Chief is the Director of this agency which operates as the Disaster Services Division of the Calgary Fire Department. The Division are responsible for peacetime disasters which entails planning, training, coordinating and evaluating individual disaster plans.

Lacombe Home Evacuation Drill.

LRT Disaster Drill.

173

Training

Preparation for an emergency requires the development of physical and mental skills that must parallel the anticipated problems. A training program is not just a "laundry list" of tasks that each individual must be capable of performing. It should reflect the entire range of techniques required to cope with potential emergencies. Out Department's ability to handle the "routine" fires is not in question, but the ability to handle a very serious situation could overtax our performance capability and this cannot be allowed to occur. If the problems have been identified properly by other elements within our system, then the proper training programs will provide potential solutions well in advance.

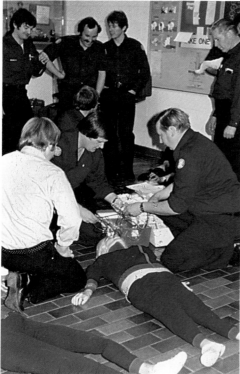

Hazardous Materials Section

The multitude of new chemicals being developed annually, compounds our apprehensions that spills or accidents involving hazardous and dangerous materials will continue to occur. Preparing for this inevitability is another of our responsibilities. By recording the whereabouts of these goods, whether in transportation or storage, we plan our response and handling procedures.

Research and Development

Nothing stays the same forever. As problems change, newer methods of solving these problems must be developed. This is the role of research and development activities within our Department. It is designed to identify areas in our organization which are deficient and to develop and analyze alternatives.

Ultimately, the comprehensive studies and analysis of our Department's future needs will be completed and a master plan will be developed from the results.
January, 1984.

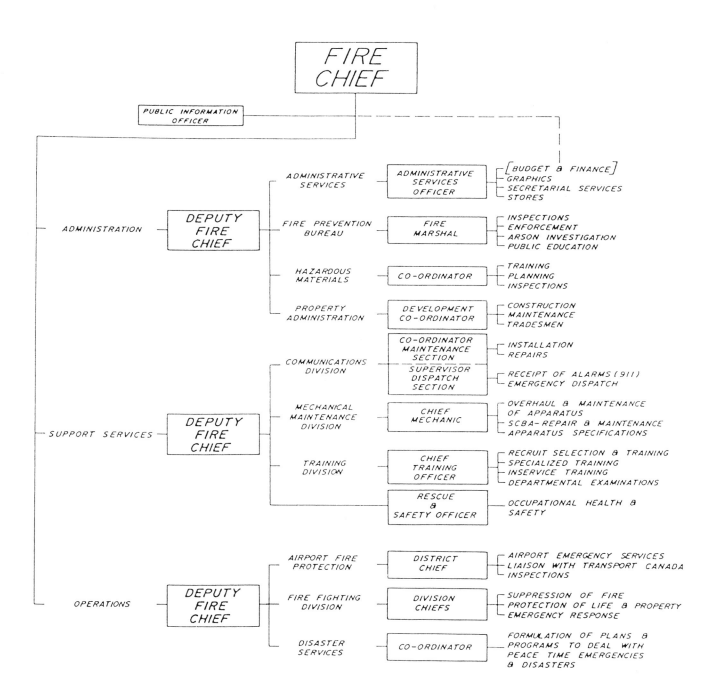

Appendix A: Fire Stations

No. 1 Fire Station, 122-7 Ave. S.E., 1887 (Demolished 1912).

No. 1 Fire Station, 450-1st S. S.E., 1973.

No. 2 Fire Station, 1801-MacLeod Tr. S.E., 1912.

No. 1 Fire Station, 138-6th Ave. S.E., 1911.

No. 2 Fire Station, 119-12th Ave. S.W., 1905.

No. 2 Fire Station, 1010-10th Ave. S.W., 1976.

178

No. 3 Fire Station, 1030-9th Ave. S.E., 1906.

No. 3 Fire Station, 2308-17th St. S.E., 1952.

No. 4 Fire Station, 104-6A St. N.E., 1907.

No. 4 Fire Station, #16 Moncton Rd. N.E., 1977.

No. 5 Fire Station, 1139-17th Ave. S.W., 1909.

No. 5 Fire Station, 1629-Scotland St. S.W., 1932.

No. 5 Fire Station, 3129-14th St. S.W., 1952.

No. 6 Fire Station, 1110-Memorial Dr. N.W., 1906.

No. 6 Fire Station, 1940-Westmount Blvd. N.W., 1964.

No. 7 Fire Station, 140-16th Ave. N.W., 1914.

No. 7 Fire Station, 2708-4th St. N.W., 1965.

No. 8 Fire Station, 10 Ave. 20th St. S.E. (Walker Est.), 1914.

No. 8 Fire Station, 2208-29th St. S.W., 1954.

No. 8 Fire Station, 1720-45th St. S.W., 1980.

No. 9 Fire Station, Ogden Rd. and 68th Ave. S.E., 1912.

No. 9 Fire Station, 6805 Ogden Rd. S.E., 1954.

No. 9 Fire Station, 2515-78th Ave. S.E., 1980.

No. 10 Fire Station, 2415-26th St. S.W., 1914.

No. 10 Fire Station, 1711-20th St. N.W., 1956.

No. 11 Fire Station, 5536-4th St. S.W., 1957.

No. 12 Fire Station, 3802-17th Ave. S.E., 1962. (Forest Lawn Annexation)

No. 12 Fire Station, 123-44th St. S.E., 1974.

No. 13 Fire Station, Calgary Int. Airport North Station, 1977.

No. 14 Fire Station, 9825-MacLeod Tr. S.E., 1963.

No. 15 Fire Station, 6328-35th Ave. N.W., 1964.

No. 16 Fire Station, 4124-11th St. S.E., 1969. Fire Headquarters.

No. 17 Fire Station, 3740-32nd Ave. N.W., 1971.

No. 18 Fire Station, 415-68th Ave. N.W., 1975.

No. 19 Fire Station, 855-Parkwood Way S.E., 1975.

No. 20 Fire Station, 5116 Richard Rd. S.W., 1978.

No. 21 Fire Station, 209-Silvergrove Dr. N.W., 1978.

No. 22 Fire Station, 7199-Temple Dr. N.E., 1979.

No. 23 Fire Station, 2727-26th Ave. S.E., 1982.

No. 24 Fire Station, 2607-106 Ave. S.W., 1981.

No. 25 Fire Station, 4705-76th Ave. S.E., 1982.

No. 26 Fire Station, 271 Midpark Blvd. S.E., 1982.

No. 27 Fire Station, Calgary Int. Airport, South Station, 1962.

Fire Training Academy, 5727-23rd Ave. S.E., 1983.

Rotary Park Dispatch Centre, 107-7th Ave. N.E., 1948.

Fire Prevention Bureau, 4124-11th St. S.E., 1974.

Fire Maintenance Shop, 4124-11th St. S.E. (Fire Headquarters), 1969.

Fire Training and Smoke House, 2308-17th St. S.W., 1958.

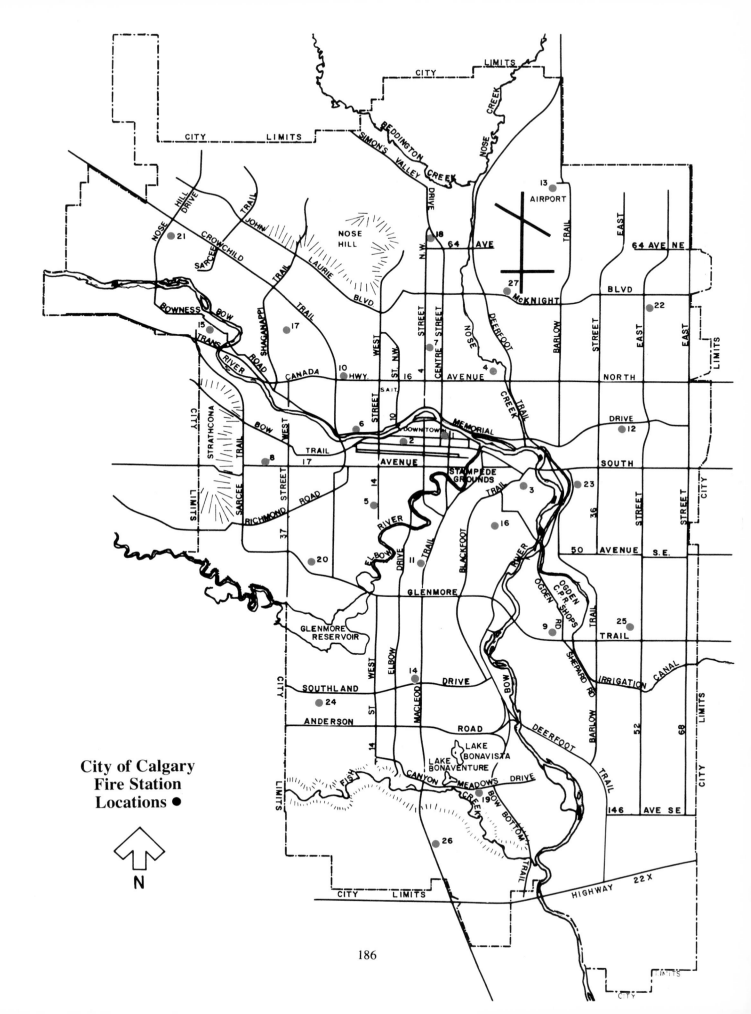

**City of Calgary
Fire Station
Locations ●**

N

Appendix B: City Outlines

Aerial view of city.

McMahon Stadium and University of Calgary.

Glenmore Reservoir and Heritage Park.

Downtown Calgary.

Saddledome and Exhibition Grounds.

Appendix C: Bigger and Better Machines

Fire Trucks/Apparatus

The "fire trucks" of the Calgary Fire Department are divided into four basic categories: pumpers, aerials, emergency rescue units, tankers.

Several "specialty" apparatus, which compliment those listed above, are strategically located throughout the city. They are: foam units, 150 foot (45 m) elevating platform (Firebird ©), parkade vehicles.

Other "support vehicles": fuel (gas) truck, auxiliaries, mobile generating plants, command vehicles, arson van, public information van, mobile repair shop, hazardous materials response units, and rescue/patrol boats.

All Fire Department emergency vehicles are equipped with: a twelve channel, U.H.F. two-way radio, a Federal Interceptor electronic siren and public address system and full compliment of breathing apparatus for all crew members.

Pumpers

Each fire station houses at least one fire pumper which is the first apparatus or lead apparatus, to respond to each emergency call in a fire district. Each of the department's fire pumpers is equipped in basically the same manner. The only differences being: the size or capacity of the fire pump (water pump) and related power train, the amount and size of fire hose that each pumper carries, and to varying degrees, the type and kind of equipment carried on each pumper.

Minimum Standard Hose Supply on Most Pumpers

— 2,000 feet of 2½″ hose (610 m of 65 mm)
— 400 feet of 1½″ hose (120 m of 38 mm) preconnected
— 50 feet of 5″ supply hose (15 m of 130 mm) preconnected

The following example typifies a Calgary Fire Department pumper:

Minimum Manpower	Power Train
Captain	gasoline or diesel powered
Senior Firefighter	automatic transmission
Driver/operator	single axle with dual wheels
Hydrant man	midship mounted fire pump, * (water pump), a 500 gallon (2200 L) water tank.

* The smallest C.F.D. pump is rated at 840 gallons per minute (4,000 L/min)
— the largest at 1,750 g.p.m. (8,000 L/min).

The "pump" is used to convey water from a source (such as a fire hydrant) and distribute it in a safe and effective manner to the nozzles of the fire hose(s).

Including reserve units and "Squad Pumpers", the department operates thirty-five fire pumpers.

Squad Pumpers

Squad Pumpers are fully crewed pumpers which are housed in four different fire stations. Usually stationed along side district pumpers, the four squads normally operate in a back-up role. Their primary responsibility is to move into fire stations, when the normal fire crew is busy at an emergency. This enables the "squad" to respond to other incidents that may occur in that district.

Their second role is to "replace" fire station crews, so that non-emergency activities, such as inspecting buildings (for fire safety) and training exercises, can be carried out by the station crews, who are confident their fire district is being adequately protected in their absence, by the Squad crew. The check sheet exemplifies the equipment on the pumpers.

Equipment Check Sheet
Apparatus #P 201

Cab — Monthly Fuel and Oil Sheet; 3 U.H.F. Radios; (#1-1, 1-2, 1-3); Fire Report; Accident Reports; Gas Removal Tags; Alarm System Notices; Portable Spotlight and Battery Pack; Hand Lamp; Pencil; 2 Pr. Driver's Gloves; 2 Demand Masks; High Rise Books 14 and 15; Set of Keys; Map Light; F.I.F.I. Book; Emergency Book; 1 Haz. Material Book; L.R.T. Book; Flashlight and Cone.
Crew Cab — 2 Demand Masks; 2 Ear Protectors.
Top Deck — 2 — Hand Lamps; 2 — 38 mm Hose Packs; 2 — 65 mm Hose Packs; Jack All Jack and Hooks; Check Tank.
2 High Rise Belts Containing — Crescent Wrench; Utility Knife; Sprinkler Tong; Uni-Driver; Wajax Spanner; Britool Spanner; Crate Bar; 3 — Door Wedges; Channel Lock Pliers; Flashlight; 5 — Door Keepers.
Left Side — Axe; Hose Control; Combination Ladder; Applicator Nozzle; Ram Nozzle; 2 — Hose Spanners; 2 m Pike Pole.
Locker #1 — Natural Gas Plug; 2 — 130 mm Spanner; Hose Reel Crank; Bolt Cutter; Rubber Mallet; Claw Hammer and Nails; Sprinkler Tong; Sprinkler Wedge; 2 Door Wedges; Pipe Wrench; Crescent Wrench; Allen Wrenches; Uni-Driver; Screwdriver; Channel Lock Pliers; Lino Knife; Hacksaw and 2 Spare Blades; Roll of Electrical Tape; Seal-All; Gas Pads; Syphon Hose; WD-40; 38 mm Plastic Nozzle; Hydrant Gate; R & L Gloves; 2 Litres Wet Water; Hose Reel Spanner; Car Entry Tool; Squirt Can; Pliers; Ejector Hook; Assorted Washers; Door Ease; Bar of Soap; Chalk; Sponge and Chamois; Bottle Methol Hydrate.
Locker #2 — 4 — 77 mm Hose.
Locker #3 — Wrecking Bar; 2 Wheel Blocks; Hall Runner; Ram Nozzle; 65 mm Wye; 65 mm-38 mm Gated Wye; Hydrant Gate; 2 m Chain.
Locker #4 — 65 mm Nozzle; 38 mm Nozzle; Jumbo Fog Nozzle; 2 — 38 mm Tips; 2 — 32 mm Tips.
Locker #5 — Demand Mask; 747 Med. Kit.
Locker #6 — Tow Chain; Hose Roller; Bag of Sawdust; 2 Hose Clamps.
Hose Bed — 600 m-65 mm Hose; 120 m-38 mm Hose; 2 — 38 mm Nozzles; Hydrant Gate; 2 Sets M & F Adaptors; 2 Hydrant Keys; 30 m-130 mm Hose; Straight 130 mm Adaptor; 60 m-65 mm Hand Line; 65 mm Nozzle.
Locker #7 — 91 m-13 mm Life Line; 60 m-10 mm Rope.
Locker #8 — Tarp; 3 Hose Ropes.
Locker #9 — 4 Disposable Blankets; Tarp; 1 L Saline.
Locker #10 — Gas Can; Pressurized Water Ext.; Indian Hand Pump.
Right Side — 7 m Extension Ladder; 4 m Roof Ladder; 3.5 m Pike Pole; 2 Hand Lamps; 2-65 mm Spanners; 14 kg. Dry Chem.; Axe.

Aerial Apparatus

The aerials of the C.F.D. are basically the same in construction and operation. Powered by a power take off (P.T.O.) from the trucks power train, the hydraulically powered, 100 foot (30 m) extension ladder is either mid-ship mounted, where the turntable is mounted directly behind the truck cab, or rear mounted, where the turn-table is situated over the rear axle.

In addition to the equipment listed on the typical aerial check sheet, each aerial ladder is provided with:

Minimum Manpower	Power Train
Lieutenant	gasoline or diesel powered
Driver/operator	automatic transmission single axle with dual wheels intercom from the turn table (where the operator stands) to the top of the aerial ladder.

The Department's fifteen aerials (including reserve units) are located throughout the city. They respond with pumpers to alarms where their need is indicated, or where their manpower can be utilized (e.g. high rise buildings).

Equipment Check Sheet
Apparatus #A-301

Cab — Monthly Fuel and Oil Sheet; 3 — UHF Radios; Fire Report Book; Accident Reports; Gas Removal Tags; Alarm System Notices; Pencil and Lamp; City Map Book; Portable Spot Light and Battery Pack; Flashlight; Driver's Mitts and Gloves; Set of Keys; F.I.F.I. Book; Map Light; 1 — Pr. Safety Glasses; Operators Manual.
Left Side — 2 — 65 mm Hose Spanners; Axe.
Locker #1 — Tool Box Containing: Uni-Driver; Screwdriver; Pipe Wrench; Crescent Wrench; Claw Hammer; Pliers; 2 — Door Wedges; Cheater; Car Entry Tool.
Locker #2 — 2 — Flood Lamps; Hand Lamp.
Locker #3 — Hydraulic Jack Handle; 1 — Ratchet Head and Ratchet for Aerial ladder; Light Plant; 4.5 Litre Gas Can Funnel; 2 — Wheel Chalks; 2 — Jack Pads.
Locker #4 — 30 m-77 mm Hose; 3 Way Siamese (65 mm).
Locker #5 — Cellar Nozzle and Hose; Hydrant Gate; 65 mm Exposure Nozzle.
Locker #6 — Jumbo Fog Nozzle; 2 — Cord Reels.
Locker #7 — 2 — Cord Reels; 2 M & F Adaptors; 10 kg Dry Chem.
Rear — Collapsible Ladder; Remote Control Ladder; 5 m Roof Ladder; 6 m Wall Ladder; 7 m Extension Ladder; 10 m Extension Ladder; 15 m Extension Ladder; 2 — 2 m Pike Poles; 2 — 2.5 m Pike Poles; 2 — 3 m Pike Poles; 2 — Hose Clamps.
Right Side, Locker #8 — 2 — Ladder Belts; 2 — Life Belts.
Locker #9 — Mop Pail; Pail; Sponge and Chamois.
Locker #10 — 2 — Tarps; Rubber and Leather Gloves; First Aid and Kit; 2 — Disposable Blankets.
Locker #11 — 45 m Stretcher Rope and Hook; 45 m Life Line; 2 — Guy Ropes; Lashing Rope; 38 m-16 mm Rope; 38 m-19 mm Rope; 12 m-Short Rope; 3 — Hose Ropes; Hose Roller.
Locker #12 — 2 — Demand Masks.
Locker #13 — 2 — Wheel Chalks; Hand Lamp; Smoke Ejector and Hook; 4 — Hose Ramps; 2 — Jack Pads.
Right Side — 2 — Spanners; Axe.
Top Deck — Play Pipe; 2 — Spanners — 44 mm, 38 mm, 32 mm; Remote Control Nozzle; 10 kg. Propane Tank and Torch and Striker; 2 — Crow Bars.
Basket Containing — 2 — Scoop Shovels; 2 — Fire Brooms; 2 — Mops; 2 — Corn Brooms; 2 — Squeegees; Sledge Hammer; Stokes Stretcher.

Emergency Rescue Units

The five "emergencies" are stationed throughout the city; one in each quadrant . . . one in the downtown area. Equipped in much the same manner, these units respond with a district pumper to alarms involving fires, cave-ins, motor vehicle accidents, high angle rescue, etc.

Minimum Manpower	Power Train
Lieutenant	gasoline or diesel powered
Driver/operator	automatic transmission single axle with dual wheels gasoline powered 110 volt generator with 200 foot (60 m) power cords on reels.

The "emergencies" have a heated crew area, where operations such as the changing of cylinders on Self Contained Breathing Apparatus, can take place in relative comfort and safety. Although the emergency rescue unit is a multi-purpose "fire truck", it is used primarily: for rescue; for salvage and overhaul; for support . . . providing emergency lighting, additional air cylinders and heavier and more diverse tools and equipment for forcible entry, fire rescue, ventilation practices, and salvage and overhaul evolutions; as a mobile repeater station for portable radio "tactical channels."

Equipment Check Sheet
Apparatus #E507

Cab — Portable Radio; Monthly Fuel and Oil Sheet; Fire Report Book; Accident Report; Alarm System Notices; Technical Data Book; Box Fuses; Radiation Monitor; 3 Prs. Gloves and Liners; Cab Jack Handle; Hand Lamp; Port. Spotlight and Battery Pack; City Map Book; Pencil; Set of Maps; Haz. Mat. Book; FIFI Book; L.R.T. Book; L.R.T. Keys; Alarm Box Ring; Heat Paste.

Locker #1 — 2 Pr. R and L Gloves; 2 Sprinkler Wedges; 2 Sprinkler Tongs; Long Hay Hook; 3 Hay Hooks; 5 Assort. Pig Tails; 11 Door Keepers; Hose Roller; Bottle of Liquid Soap; Car Entry Tool; Coat Hanger; Oil Can; Rubber Mallet; 2 Wheel Wrenches; Pry Axe; Can of Nails; Syphon Hose; Utility Knife; 23 pc. ½" Drive Socket.

Tool Box — 2 Ball Peen Hammers; Grease Gun; Claw Hammer; Lino Knife; Crescent Wrench; Pipe Wrench; 2 Screwdrivers; Uni-Driver; 2 Pliers; Channel Lock Pliers; Needle Nose Pliers; Side Cutters; Tin Snips; Hacksaw and 3 sp. Blades; 38 mm Spanner; Seal All; 5 Cold Chisels; Pry Punch Bar; Spare Spark Plugs (3); Natural Gas Plug; Cutting Torch Cleaner; Deep Socket Set; 7 pc. Comb. Wrenches; Electrical Tape; Crate Bar.

Locker #2 — 24 "S" Hooks; 20 Door Wedges; 9 Hose Ropes; 4 Ejector Hooks; 6 Lengths 38 mm Hose.

Locker #3 — 2 Sump Pumps; 4 Short Ropes.

Locker #4 — 2 Ear Protectors; Smoke Ejector and Socks; 2 Thorn Lights; Jack all Jack; K-12 Saw and Blades and Wrenches; 2 Pr. Leather Gloves.

Locker #5 — 6 Cans 3% Foam; Foam Inductor; Foam Playpipe.

Locker #6 — Hand Lamp; 3 Smoke Ejectors.

Locker #7 — 4 Mops; 4 Squeegees; 2 Corn Brooms; 2 Hay Forks; 4 Scoop Shovels; 1 Round Nosed Shovel; 2 Stable Brooms; Bag of Sawdust.

Locker #8 — 2 Meter Pike Poles; 2 Bags of Sawdust; 3 Fracture Boards; 5' Telescoping Ladder; Stoke Stretcher and Sling; Water Shut-off Key; Gas Shut-off Key; Hot Stick.

Locker #9 — 3 Mop Pails; 2 Pails; 2 Vacuum Hoses; 5 Assort. Vacuum Heads; 2 Vacuum Wands.

Locker #10 — 2 Gas Cans; Funnel; Starter Rope; Chain Saw; Can of Hurst Hyd. Fluid.

Locker #11 — 2 Wheel Blocks; 11 Tonne Jack and Handle; Come Along; Jet Puller.

Locker #12 — 8 Cords Reels; Hand Lamp; 4 Flood Lamps.

Locker #13 — Cutting Torch and Cart; Leather Gloves; Aluminized Blanket; Striker, Goggles.

Locker #14 — Hurst Tool and Motor; Hurst Cutter and Hose; 2 Pr. Gauntlet Gloves; 2 Thorn Lights; Safety Goggles.

Locker #15 — Hurst Equipment: 3 Chains; 2 Mallets; 2 Hooks; 2 Tips; 2 Metal Dowels; 2 Metal Ripper Teeth; Plastic Dowel Driver.

Locker #16 — 18 Wooden Blocks; Set of Flares; Ajax Tool; Mini Grinder; Tow Chain.

Crew Cab — Left Locker: 8 Disp Blankets; Water/Sewer/Gas/Line Maps; 747 First Aid Kit; 16 mm Lifeline 91 m.

Right Centre — 4 Tarps; 2 Hallrunners; 1 Sump Pump Pan.

Right Locker — 5 Vetter Bags; Shutoff Valves; 2 Hoses, tanks and Reg. Control; Life Belt; 30 m-19 mm Rope; 30 m-13 mm Rope; 91 m-11 mm Rope; 91 m-16 mm Rope.

Under Long Seat — 2 Pr. Rubber Boots; 2 Pr. Hip Waders; 12 Chemox Cann.; Roll of Poly; Can of Staples; Stapler; Bundle of Lath; Hand Saw; 38 mm Plast. Noz.; 38 mm Fog Nozzle; 65-38 mm Gated Wye; Hammer Stapler; ⅜" Staples; 3 Traffic Lights.

Demand Tank Lockers — 32 Demand Tanks; 4 Demand Masks.

Crew Cab Floor — Indian Hand Pump; Wet/Dry Vacuum; Dust Bag; 10 kg. Dry. Chem. Ext.; 14 kg. Dry Chem. Ext.; 5 Chemox Masks; 4 Thorn Ballasts; 6 Port. Radios and Cases.

Wooden Box — 2 Axes; Kelly Tool; Sledge Hammer; Crow Bar; Wrecking Bar; Utility Bar; Tin Roof Cutter; Bolt Cutter; 6 Rolls of Ribbon.

Tankers

The department's five tankers are housed in fire stations which are located near to the City's perimeter.

Their primary function is to transport water to areas where water supplies are either limited or are too far from the emergency scene to be effective. Rural districts and areas along the "free way systems" (i.e. the Deerfoot Trail) are such areas.

Minimum Manpower	Power Train
Lieutenant	gasoline or diesel powered
Driver/operator	automatic transmission single axle with dual wheels or tandem axle with dual wheels

The tankers are equipped with a P.T.O. powered, midship mounted pump, which enables them to fight fires, usually grass or brush fires, as well as for transferring water to other apparatus (e.g. a fire pumper).

A portable pump is carried on each tanker, this allows the crew to obtain water (their third respon-

sibility, when the need arises, from swimming pools, creeks, sloughs, cisterns, etc.

The tankers respond with a district pumper; their crews supplementing manpower needs when the tanker itself, is not needed.

The capacity of the smallest tanker is 1,000 gallons (4,500 L), weighing approximately 10,000 pounds (4,500 kg).

The capacity of the largest tanker (a tandem) is 1,800 gallons (8,200 L), which weighs approximately nine tons (8.1 tonnes).

Equipment Check Sheet
Apparatus #T405

Cab — Monthly Fuel and Oil Sheet; First Aid Kit; City Map Book; Accident Report; Flashlight; Safety Goggles; Fire Report Book; Hand Lamp; Sponge and Chamois; Map Box and Maps; Set of Keys; F.I.F.I. Book; Spotlight and Battery Pack; Portable Radio.

Locker #1 — 9 — Cans AFFF 3%; 4 L Methyl Hydrate; 4 — Fire Brooms; 1 — Mop; 2 — Corn Brooms; 3 L Wet Water; 4.5 Litres Fire Stream Plus.

Locker #2 — Tool Box Containing: Allen Wrenches; Uni-Driver; Lino Knife; Pliers; Screwdriver; File; Hacksaw and 2 Spare Blades; Channel Lock Pliers; Crescent Wrench; Claw Hammer; Rubber Mallet; Assorted Washers; Seal-All; Gas Pads; 2 — Hay Hooks; Car Entry Tool; Hand Lamp; Simon Valley Hyd. Key; Squirt Can Methyl Hydrat; 2 Bags Sawdust.

Locker #3 — 2 — Wheel Chalks.

Locker #4 — 2 — Demand Masks.

Locker #5 — 2 — Spare Demand Tanks; 3 — Hose Ropes; 23 m-19 mm Rope.

Locker #6 — Axe; 2 — Hose Clamps.

Locker #7 — 14 kg. Dry Chem. Ext.; Axe; Tow Chain.

Locker #8 — Hand Pump; Pail; Mop Pail; Funnel.

Left Side — 2 — Spanners; 2 — 77 mm Hard Suctions and Strainer; 38 mm Pre-Connect; 77 mm-65 mm Adaptor.

Locker #9 — 2 Litre 2 Cycle Oil; Portable Pump; 38 mm Hose; 65 mm Pony; 2 — Gas Cans; Float Dock Strainer; 65 mm Filler Hose.

Top Deck — 4 — 65 mm Hose; Scoop Shovel; Square Nosed Shovel; 2 — Round Nosed Shovels; 2 — Hay Forks; 90 m-38 mm Hose; 2 — 38 mm Nozzles; 2 — Squeegees; 2 — 77 mm Hard Suction.

Right Side — 7 m Extension Ladder; Applicator and Shut-Off; 2 m Pike Pole.

Locker #10 — Hand Pump; Indian Hand Pump.

Locker #11 — 65 mm-38 mm Wye; Hydrant Gate; 2 — Hydrant Keys; 38 mm Fog Nozzle; 2 — 38 mm Plastic Nozzles; 1 — Set M & F Adaptors.

Locker #12 — Wrecking Bar; Bolt Cutters; Utility Bar.

Locker #13 — Foam Inductor and Want.

Locker #14 — Hand Lamp; R and L Gloves; Suction Strainer Rope.

Locker #15 — 45 m-65 mm Hose; 65 mm Nozzle.

The apparatus and vehicles of the Calgary Fire Department are catalogued with identification numbers known as "shop numbers". The fire apparatus also have station identity numbers that are used in the everyday duties of firefighting.

Five pumpers that are housed in stations that form an inner city perimeter, are equipped with 1,000 feet (305 m) of 5 inch hose (130 mm). They have both 5 inch intakes and outlets which allows these pumps to move at least 1,000 gallons of water per minute . . . from any hydrant. These units are equipped with "deck guns" that are pre-piped, which allows for an almost immediate defensive or offensive attack. The hose is equipped with Storz© quick connect couplings and because of the hoses synthetic make up, it can be loaded wet, a great advantage over the cotton jacketed "older hose". The five fire stations that house these pumpers are: Number Six, Number Eight (squad), Number Eleven, Number Twenty-two and Number Twenty-five.

Number One Station Pumper: Number of like pumpers on this department — 5
— Hendrickson chassis, powered by a 350 H.P. diesel engine
— Automatic Transmission
— Water tank capacity — 460 gallons (2,100 L)
— Pump capacity — 1,750 gallons per minute (8,000 L/min)

Number Sixteen Station Pumper: Number of like pumpers on this department — 1
— Hendrickson chassis, powered by a 350 H.P. diesel engine
— Automatic transmission
— Water tank capacity — 500 gallons (2,270 L)
— Pump capacity — 1,500 gallons per minute (6,800 L/min)
   These units are equipped with an elevating nozzle tower (articulating arm) which can reach a height of 54 feet (16.4 m). The nozzle has a capacity of 840 gallons per minute (3,800 L/min). The unit is known as a "Squrt"©.

Number Four Station Pumper: Number of like pumpers on this department — 1
— International chassis, powered by a 265 H.P. diesel engine
— Automatic transmission
— Water tank capacity — 500 gallons (2,270 L)
— Pump capacity — 1,050 gallons per minute (4,800 L/min)
   This unit also has an elevating tower nozzle (articulating arm) which can reach a height of 54 feet (16.4 m). The nozzle has a capacity of 840 gallons per minute (3,800 L/min). The unit is known as a "Squrt"©.

Number Sixteen Station Squad Pumper: Number of like pumpers on this department — 14
— International chassis, powered by a 265 H.P. diesel engine
— Automatic transmission
— Water tank capacity — 500 gallons (2,270 L)
— Pump capacity — 1,050 gallons per minute (4,800 L/min)

Number Four Station Squad-Pumper: Number of like units on this department — 4
— International chassis, powered by a 210 H.P. diesel engine
— Automatic transmission
— Water tank capcity — 500 gallons (2,270 L)
— Pump capacity — 840 gallons per minute (3,800 L/min)

Number Twenty-Seven Station Pumper: Number of like units on this department — 2
— G.M.C. chassis, powered by a 275 H.P. gasoline engine
— Five speed, manual transmission
— Water tank capacity — 500 gallons (2,270 L)
— Pump capacity — 1,050 gallons per minute (4,800 L/min)

Number Twenty-Six Station Pumper: Number of like units on this department — 4
— International Chassis, powered by a 285 H.P. gasoline engine
— Five speed, manual transmission
— Water tank capacity — 500 gallons (2,270 L)
— Pump capacity — 1,050 gallons per minute (4,800 L/min)

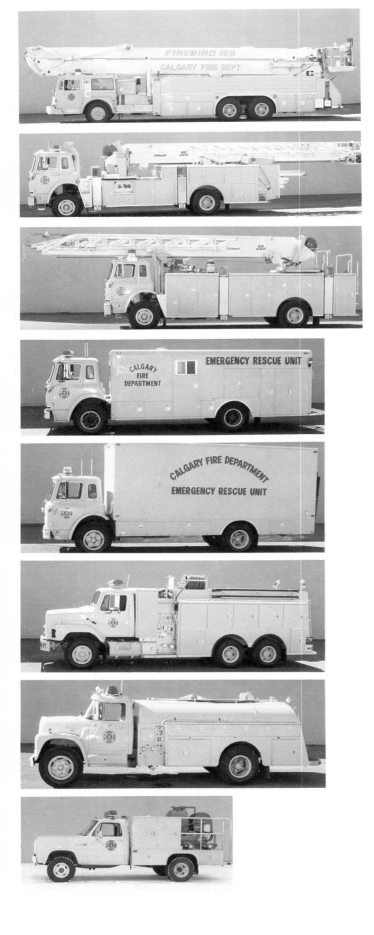

Number Two Station Firebird ©: Number of like units on this department — 1
— Firebird chassis by Calavar© powered by a diesel engine
— Automatic transmission
— 150 foot elevating platform (45 m) with a load capacity of 750 pounds (340 kg), reaches highest of any elevating platform available in North America.
— The Firebird is used for:
— firefighting, fire rescues and other rescue work
— a water tower, using its built in water piping system
— an observation platform with piped air supply for the operator's breathing apparatus
— ventilation procedures in burning buildings
— provides external access to high places for firefighters and equipment
— also carries a wide variety of "hand ladders"
  The length of this truck is 46.5 feet (14.2 m) and its height is 12 feet (3.6 m). When the units outrigger, stabilizing jacks are extended, the unit is 24 feet wide (7.3 m). The unit weights 66,000 pounds, (33 tons) (30 tonnes).

Number Twenty-One Station Aerial: Number of like units on this department — 10
— International chassis, powered by a gasoline engine
— midship mounted, hydraulically operated, 100 foot (30 m) aerial extension ladder
— carries a wide variety of "hand ladders" up to 50 feet (15 m)

Number Six Station Aerial: Number of like units on this department — 5
— Scott or International chassis, powered by a diesel engine
— automatic transmission
— rear mounted, hydraulically operated, 100 foot (30 m) aerial extension ladder
— carries a wide variety of "hand ladders" up to 50 feet (15 m)

Number Sixteen Station Emergency: Number of like units on this department — 4
— International chassis, powered by either diesel or gasoline engine
— automatic transmission

Number Two Emergency: Number of like units on this department — 1
— International chassis, powered by a diesel engine
— automatic transmission
  This unit, as well as being equipped like the other Emergency Rescue Units, has much of its equipment "containerized", which allows it to be "dollied" to the upper floors of high rise buildings, which it primarily responds to.

Number Twenty-Six Station Tanker: Number of like units on this department — 2
— International tandem chassis, powered by a 330 H.P. diesel engine
— automatic transmission
— 1,800 gallon tank (8,182 L)

Number Twenty-Two Station Tanker: Number of like units on this department — 4
— International chassis, powered by a 200 H.P. gasoline engine
— standard transmission
— 1,000 gallon tank (4,500 L)

Number One Station Twin Agent Foam Unit: Number of like units on this department — 1
— Dodge One ton chassis, 4x4
  This unit is used for quick attacks on petroleum based fires, usually the result of motor vehicle accidents or spills.
  Nitrogen under pressure is used to pressurize a 450 pound (204 kg) container of dry chemical powder and a second container of foam solution, which is then discharged through twin hose lines to form a highly effective fire extinguisher. Although this unit can be put into operation with one man, a two man crew is preferred.

Number Nine Station Foam Fire Fighter: Number of like units on this department — 1
— Dodge one ton chassis, 4x4

This unit carries 240 gallons (1,091 L) of high concentration foam. It operates in conjunction with a pumper. It will mix the prescribe amount of concentrate to produce an effective foam fire-fighting agent . . . for petroleum based fires.

Number Two Station Parkade Vehicle: Number of like units on this department — 1
— International Scout chassis, 4x4

This unit carries water, foam concentrate and portable extinguishers. It is used primarily for fighting fires in areas a pumper could not go. Particularly useful in underground parkades.

Number One Station Rescue: Number of like units on this department — 1
— Dodge one ton chassis
— automatic transmission

This unit is used extensively in river rescue work. Carries a flotation device known as the Res-Q-Dek © which is used for conducting water rescues in fast moving water. The units locker space is used for carrying diving equipment. The Res-Q-Dek consists of 2 — 12 foot (3.65 m) Goodyear Rubber inflatable pontoons which are connected by an aluminum folding cat-walk. It is powered by a 25 H.P. Mercury long shaft outboard motor with a propeller drive. The "dek" will carry 10,000 pounds (4,500 kg).

Number One Station Rescue/Patrol Boat: (B-801)
— Twenty-four foot (7.3 m) Performance Craft steel bottom river boat
— Eight foot (2.43 m) beam, 14 gauge steel bottom
— weight = 3,500 lbs (1,600 kg)
— Built by C.C.O. Marine in Red Deer, Alberta
— Powered by a 455 cu.in. Oldsmobile, 285 H.P. low compression engine (in board) with a Jacuzzi jet drive (80 p.s.i. at 3,200 R.P.M.s)
— The boat will hold a maximum fifteen people, carries 65 gallons of number two gasoline (about 10 gallons per hour) and will draft about 9 inches of water.

Number One Station Rescue/Patrol Boat: (B-806)
— Twenty-two foot (6.7 m) Almar aluminum River Boat
— Built by Almar Marine Construction, Tacoma, Washington
— Powered by a 454 cu. in. Mercury inboard with a 3 stage Hamilton Jet Drive
— This boat was donated to the Calgary Fire Department by the Alberta Provincial Government.

Number Twenty-Six Station Rescue/Patrol Boat: (B-802)
— Seventeen foot, five inch Zodiac Mark IV grande raid inflatable
— Powered by a 50 H.P. Mercury Outboard engine with a jet drive

Number Twenty-Six Station Rescue/Patrol Boat: (B-805)
— Eleven foot, six inch Bombard C-3 inflatable
— Powered by a 25 H.P. Mercury Outboard engine with a propeller drive.

195

Support Apparatus

Mobile Gas Truck.

Auxiliary Unit.

Mobile Generating Plant.

Command Vehicle.

Command Vehicle.

Mask Maze, Mobile Training Unit.

Public Information Vehicle.

Mobile Repair Vehicle.

Hazardous Materials Response Unit.

Hazardous Materials Response Unit.

Fire/Police Arson Van.

Fire Dept. Passenger Bus.

M.O.T. Apparatus Assigned to Airport Operations

Number Thirteen and Twenty-Seven: Airport Stations (M.O.T.)
Red Two:
— Dry Chemical Unit
— International 4x4 chassis
— 1000 pounds (450 kg) of dry chemical powder
— Nitrogen Cylinders, pressure from which, is used to expell the powder as well as operate a variety of power tools which are used to force entry into aircraft.

Red Three and Red Four (two units):
— Foam Boss©
— Powered by a 600 H.P. diesel engine
— pump is powered by an auxiliary engine (allows operator to pump foam while manouvering the unit)
   This unit carries 2,000 gallons (9,100 L) of water and 160 gallons (725 L) of foam concentrate. The units are used primarily for aircraft crash/rescue.

Red Six:
— Tanker
— F.W.D. chassis
— Powered by a 534 cubic inch (8.75 L) 275 H.P. engine
— Automatic transmission
— Pump is powered by an auxiliary engine.
   This unit carries 2,000 gallons (9,100 L) of water and 180 gallons (820 L) of foam concentrate.

Red Five:
— Airport Utility Vehicle
— Jeep
— Used also for Parkade Incidents.

January 1, 1984, Calgary Fire Department Ambulance Division was separated from this department and is now the City of Calgary Emergency Medical Services.

Emergency Medical Services Units

Emergency Paramedic Ambulance: Number of like units — 19:
— 460 CI engine.
— Automatic Transmission
— Full complement of equipment to handle all medical incidents
— Complement of at least one Paramedic and one E.M.T. per Ambulance.

Supply and Service Vehicle: Number of like units — 1:
— 351 C.I. Gasoline Engine
— Automatic Transmission
— Used for equipment supply to all units requiring replacement of Ambulance supplies.

Mobile Intensive Care Nursery Unit: Number of like units — 1:
— 460 C.I. Gasoline
— Automatic Transmission
— Full complement of equipment to handle all transportation of new born infants to or from various locations or hospitals as required
— This vehicle was donated to the University School of Medicine by the Calgary Shriners Club and The Knights of Columbus and The Provincial Government.

A Granddaughter Writes About The Author
by Fiona Foran

Grandfather Grant MacEwan was born on August 12, 1902 near Brandon, and lived later at Melfort, Saskatchewan. His mother, Bertha Grant, was a direct descendant of James Grant who came to Nova Scotia on the ship "Hector" in 1773. He married Phyllis Cline in 1935. She, my grandmother, was a schoolteacher from Churchbridge, Saskatchewan and they had one daughter Heather, who presently lives with her family at Priddis.

Following primary school years in Saskatchewan, Grant MacEwan attended the Ontario Agricultural College at Guelph, graduating with a B.S.A. degree in 1926. Subsequently he earned his M.Sc. from the prestigious Iowa State University. Today, he holds five honorary doctorates from the Universities of Calgary (1967), Alberta (1966), Brandon (1969), Guelph (1972) and Saskatchewan (1974).

Grant MacEwan joined the faculty at the University of Saskatchewan in 1928 and over the next eighteen years, acquired a national reputation as an authority on animal husbandry. With his friend and colleague, Allister Ewen, he co-authored two pioneer textbooks, *Canadian Animal Husbandry*, and *General Agriculture*. He also authored two other technical works on agriculture, *Breeds of Livestock in Canada*, and *Feeding Farm Animals*. It was in Saskatchewan also that he developed a lasting reputation as one of western Canada's leading livestock judges.

The Sasktchewan years were crucial in developing inter-personal skills. They said he was a good teacher and former students still speak of his magic in the classroom. They remember his patience, thoroughness, understanding and above all his facility for making the most sterile subjects interesting and even memorable. He was in large measure instrumental in cementing a close and viable relationship between the University of Saskatchewan and the rural communities it served.

By the mid 1940's this man enjoyed a national reputation as an agriculturalist. He had extended his writing activities to journals, newspapers and professional magazines. Thus it was not surprising that in 1946 he was offered the position of Dean of Agriculture at the University of Manitoba, a post he accepted and held for six years before resigning in 1951. The decision to leave university life was difficult and linked with his growing public image which had manifested itself in an offer to contest the federal seat for Brandon in a by-election precipitated by the death of encumbent L. Matthews. Following his defeat at the polls in June 1951, Grant MacEwan moved to Calgary to begin a new life and new career.

In Calgary he entered civic politics as an alderman in 1953 and served nine years in that capacity before being elected mayor of Canada's fastest growing city in the fall of 1963. Between 1955 and 1959 he was also a member of the Legislative Assembly and for a time was the Leader of the Official Opposition. This experience, plus his three year stint in the mayor's chair enhanced his public image while earning a reputation as a tough, commonsensical politician.

In 1965 he was invited by Lester B. Pearson, Prime Minister of Canada to become Lieutenant Governor of Alberta. He took office on January 6, 1966 and remained eight and one half years before leaving the office on July 1, 1974.

In his role as Lieutenant Governor, he made a special effort to take the office to rural and remote parts of the province. Statistics reveal that he averaged well over a public function a day, seven days a week for eight and a half years. His travels accounted for over a quarter million miles on the official limousine, not to mention countless bus, train and air trips to include almost every village and hamlet in Alberta.

In the years following his removal from University life, Grant MacEwan became one of Western Canada's most enthusiastic historians. His concept of history has been personality oriented. He wanted to document the uniqueness of the human spirit through its basis in historical fact. Whether it be through characters like Bob Edwards, self-made men like Pat Burns, great Indians like Tatanga Mani, or through individual Metis, cattlemen, politicians, farmers or ladies, grandfather MacEwan has consistently emphasized the human dimension.

At the same time he has used history to indicate man's waywardness. He is an ardent conservationist and animal lover and abhors cruelty, waste and misuse of the environment. This concern is explicit in his most serious work, *Entrusted To My Care*.

Grant MacEwan's place in Western Canadian society is evidenced by a continuing popularity. He holds numerous awards including the Order of Canada, the first Premier's Award of Excellence, and countless citizenship and special achievement awards. He is still a much-in-demand after-dinner speaker and delivers upwards of one hundred such addressess annually as public service.

He walked more than one thousand miles in Miles for Millions and other charity walkathons, almost always surrounded by young people. A suburb in Calgary and a Community College in Edmonton bear his name, while the University of Calgary students chose to name their student building after him. Old timers frequently see him at their hospital bedsides and neighbors often find their sidewalks cleared of snow at an early morning hour.

Above all else, Grant MacEwan, has come to be seen as one who is at peace with himself and the world in an age of dependence, frustration and insecurity. He classes all creatures as his brothers and sisters and attempts to translate this belief into practice. He lives simply, frugally and by a code he has worked through himself, and if a granddaughter may judge, he has found the secrets to good and useful living.

Fiona Foran

Honorary Fire Chief
Grant MacEwan

At an official ceremony at City Hall on August 2nd, 1984, Mayor Ralph Klein and Fire Chief Tom Minhinnett bestowed upon Grant MacEwan the title of Honorary Fire Chief. A Chief's helmet and inscription, commemorating this honor, were presented to him, along with the department's appreciation for his contributions to our Centennial Book.

Lieutenant Brent Pedersen, President of the Calgary Firefighters Association, Local 255 I.A.F.F., presented Dr. MacEwan with a plaque electing him an honorary member of the Local.

PRESENTED BY FIRE CHIEF THOMAS E. MINHINNETT TO

DR. J.W. (GRANT) MacEWAN

IN RECOGNITION OF HIS CONTRIBUTIONS TO
THE HISTORY OF THE CALGARY FIRE DEPARTMENT
"100 YEARS OF SMOKE SWEAT AND TEARS"

JULY 16, 1984

Grant MacEwan, Honorary Fire Chief, August 2, 1984.

City Centre.